Tennessee Legal Research

CAROLINA ACADEMIC PRESS
LEGAL RESEARCH SERIES

Suzanne E. Rowe, Series Editor

Arkansas Legal Research
Coleen M. Barger

❧

Florida Legal Research, Third Edition
Barbara J. Busharis & Suzanne E. Rowe

❧

Georgia Legal Research
Nancy P. Johnson, Elizabeth G. Adelman, & Nancy J. Adams

❧

Illinois Legal Research
Mark E. Wojcik

❧

Michigan Legal Research
Pamela Lysaght

❧

Missouri Legal Research
Wanda M. Temm & Julie M. Cheslik

❧

Oregon Legal Research, Second Edition
Suzanne E. Rowe

❧

Pennsylvania Legal Research
Barbara J. Busharis & Bonny L. Tavares

❧

Tennessee Legal Research
Sibyl Marshall & Carol McCrehan Parker

❧

Washington Legal Research
Julie Heintz

Tennessee Legal Research

Sibyl Marshall
University of Tennessee
College of Law

Carol McCrehan Parker
University of Tennessee
College of Law

Suzanne E. Rowe, Series Editor

CAROLINA ACADEMIC PRESS
Durham, North Carolina

Library of Congress Cataloging-in-Publication Data

Marshall, Sibyl.
 Tennessee legal research / by Sibyl Marshall, Carol McCrehan
Parker.
     p. cm. -- (Carolina Academic Press legal research series)
 Includes bibliographical references and index.
 ISBN-13: 978-1-59460-347-1 (alk. paper)
 ISBN-10: 1-59460-347-2 (alk. paper)
 1. Legal research--Tennessee. I. Parker, Carol. II. Title. III. Se-
ries.

 KFT75.M37 2007
 340.072'0768--dc22

                                                    2007009172

                    CAROLINA ACADEMIC PRESS
                         700 Kent Street
                  Durham, North Carolina 27701
                   Telephone (919) 489-7486
                        Fax (919) 493-5668
                        www.cap-press.com

             Printed in the United States of America

to Jean Moore, our friend and colleague

Summary of Contents

Contents

List of Tables

Series Note

The Legal Research Series published by Carolina Academic Press includes an increasing number of titles from states around the country. The goal of each book is to provide law students, practitioners, paralegals, college students, and laypeople with the essential elements of legal research in each state. Unlike more bibliographic texts, the Legal Research Series books seek to explain concisely both the sources of state law research and the process for conducting legal research effectively.

Acknowledgments

This work, as part of a series of state legal research texts, draws on *Oregon Legal Research* for much of its organization and content, and we thank Suzanne Rowe for permission to draw on her excellent and inspiring work. We also thank our supportive and insightful colleagues at the University of Tennessee College of Law, with special thanks to Patti Ogden for her technical wizardry and crack citation formatting skills; to Reba Best, Cheryn Picquet, and Loretta Price, for guidance on numerous questions of style and substance; and to Jean Moore for her keen and careful work in reviewing and commenting on several of the chapters. Our series editor, Suzanne Rowe, not only allowed us to draw from her book but made this work immeasurably better through her editing. Finally, research assistants Corinne Martin and Harvey Rogers worked painstakingly and diligently in proofreading, verifying, correcting, and updating the manuscript and we gratefully acknowledge their help.

Tennessee Legal Research

Chapter 1

The Research Process and Legal Analysis

I. Tennessee Legal Research

The fundamentals of legal research are the same in every American jurisdiction, though the details vary. While some variations are minor, others require specialized knowledge of the resources available and the analytical framework in which those resources are used. This book focuses on the resources and analysis required to be thorough and effective in researching Tennessee law. It supplements this focus with brief explanations of federal research and research into the law of other states, both to introduce those resources and to highlight some of the variations.

II. The Intersection of Legal Research and Legal Analysis

Most students realize during the first week of law school that legal analysis is difficult. At the same time, some consider legal research simplistic busy work. The basic process of legal research *is* simple. For most online research, you will search particular websites or databases using words likely to appear in the text of relevant documents. For most print resources, you will begin with an index, find entries that appear relevant, read those sections of the text, and then find out whether more recent information is available.

Legal analysis is interwoven throughout this process, raising challenging questions. In online research, how will you choose relevant words and construct a search most likely to produce the documents you need? In print research, which words will you look up in the index? How will you decide whether an index entry looks promising? When you read a document, how will you determine whether it is relevant to your client's situation? How will you learn whether more recent material changed the law or merely applied it in a new situation? The answer to each of these questions requires legal analysis. This intersection of research and analysis can make legal research very difficult, especially for the novice. While this book's focus is legal research, it also includes the fundamental aspects of legal analysis required to conduct research competently.

This book is not designed to be a blueprint of every resource in the law library or search engine on the Internet. This book is more like a manual or field guide, introducing the types of resources needed at each step of the research process and explaining how to use them.

III. Types of Legal Authority

Before researching the law, you must be clear about the goal of your search. In most situations, you will be looking for authority that is both *primary* and *mandatory*: the constitutional provisions, statutes, procedural rules, administrative regulations, and/or judicial opinions that are binding on your client's legal issues.

Legal authority is often divided along two lines. *Primary authority* is produced by government bodies with law-making power, and it *is* the law. Legislatures write statutes, courts write judicial opinions, and administrative agencies write regulations. By contrast, *secondary authorities* are materials that are written *about* the law. Secondary authorities include treatises, law review articles, and legal encyclopedias.

Secondary authorities are designed to aid researchers in understanding the law and in locating primary authorities.[1]

Primary authority may be either *mandatory* or *persuasive* while secondary authority is always treated as persuasive, not mandatory. *Mandatory authority* is binding on the court that would decide a conflict if the situation were litigated. In a question of Tennessee law, mandatory or binding authority includes Tennessee's constitution, statutes enacted by the Tennessee legislature, opinions of the Tennessee Supreme Court,[2] and Tennessee administrative regulations. *Persuasive authority* is not binding, but may be followed if relevant and well reasoned. Primary authority is considered persuasive if it is from a different jurisdiction, or if it addresses an issue similar to, but not the same as, the issue in the case under consideration. In a question of Tennessee law, examples of persuasive authority include a similar Georgia statute, an opinion of a Kentucky state court, and a law review article. Table 1-1 shows examples of different types of authorities in Tennessee research.

Table 1-1. Examples of Authority in Tennessee Research

	Mandatory Authority	Persuasive Authority
Primary Authority	Tennessee statutes Tennessee Supreme Court cases	Georgia statutes Kentucky Supreme Court cases
Secondary Authority	———	Law review articles Legal encyclopedias

Within primary, mandatory authority, there is an interlocking hierarchy of law involving constitutions, statutes, procedural rules, ad-

---

1. A third type of legal material is the *tertiary authority* or "finding aid." These materials consist entirely of tables, indexes, digests, and citators. They are used entirely for locating primary and secondary authorities.

2. An opinion from the Tennessee Court of Criminal Appeals or the Tennessee Court of Appeals is binding on the Tennessee trial courts if the Tennessee Supreme Court has not addressed a particular issue.

ministrative regulations, and judicial opinions. The constitution of each state is the supreme law of that state. If a statute is on point, that statute comes next in the hierarchy, followed by administrative regulations and procedural rules. Courts determine whether statutes, regulations, and rules violate the constitution and will strike down any law, rule, or regulation found to be unconstitutional. Courts are also responsible for interpreting statutes, rules, and regulations, as well as ensuring that rules and regulations do not contradict statutes. If there is no constitutional provision, statute, procedural rule, or administrative regulation on point, the issue will be controlled by *common law* (judge-made law).

IV. Court Systems

Because much legal research includes reading judicial opinions, researchers need to understand the court system. The basic court structure includes a trial court, an intermediate court of appeals, and an ultimate appellate court, often called the "supreme" court. These court systems exist at both the state and federal levels.

A. Tennessee Courts

In Tennessee, there are four different types of trial level courts. Where a case will first be heard may depend on the type of case, the amount of damages sought, or the county where it is filed, as not all counties have all types of courts. *Circuit courts* are the most common type of trial courts, and they hear certain civil matters, domestic relations cases, and criminal cases. *Chancery courts* hear some family law cases and those civil cases that are traditionally considered to arise from equity rather than law.[3] The jurisdiction of the Chancery courts

---

3. *Gibson's Suits in Chancery* (William H. Inman rev., LexisNexis 2004) is considered the definitive work on theory of and practice in Tennessee chancery courts, and is highly recommended to anyone needing more in-depth information on proceeding in Tennessee chancery courts.

is varied and includes cases arising out of boundary disputes, demands for specific performance of a contract, and suits by wards against their guardians. *Criminal courts* hear exclusively criminal cases, and *Probate courts* hear cases involving wills, administration of estates, conservatorships, and guardianships.

Courts of limited jurisdiction are trial courts that typically hear smaller cases and are funded at the county level rather than the state level. In Tennessee, courts of limited jurisdiction include Juvenile courts, General Sessions courts, and Municipal courts. Again, not every county will have all of these different types of courts. Juvenile courts hear cases involving juveniles, including paternity cases, mental health cases, and juvenile delinquency cases. General Sessions courts handle preliminary hearings in criminal cases, small claims matters, traffic violations, and some civil and misdemeanor criminal matters. Municipal courts deal with preliminary hearings, traffic violations, and other misdemeanor criminal violations.

Tennessee has two intermediate courts of appeal. The Court of Criminal Appeals hears appeals in criminal cases and is required to review all death penalty sentences. The Court of Appeals hears appeals in civil cases, as well as taking appeals from certain state boards and commissions. Both intermediate courts are composed of twelve judges, who sit in panels of three in Jackson, Nashville, and Knoxville. The Tennessee Supreme Court is composed of five justices, who sit *en banc* to hear all cases. The Supreme Court also convenes regularly in Jackson, Nashville, and Knoxville.[4] The Supreme Court decides which appeals it wants to hear and is required to review only those cases where the Court of Criminal Appeals has affirmed a death sentence. The Supreme Court may also choose to assume jurisdiction over cases in the Court of Appeals or Court of Criminal Appeals if there is a particular need for a swift resolution.

---

4. Although the Court of Appeals, Court of Criminal Appeals, and Supreme Court usually are held in traditional court buildings, the courts do occasionally convene and hear argument outside of the usual courtrooms — usually at Tennessee law schools. Law students in Tennessee who are fortunate enough to have a court conducted at their law school are well advised to take advantage of this opportunity to watch the court in session.

The web site for the Tennessee judiciary is www.tsc.state.tn.us. It contains a wealth of information, including searchable databases of Tennessee court opinions, links to procedural rules and the Tennessee code, contact information for Tennessee court clerks, court forms, a self-help center, an extensive section of links to external sources on Tennessee and American law, and a series of streaming videos on basic court procedures, offered in seven languages.

B. Federal Courts

In the federal judicial system, the trial courts are called the United States District Courts. There are ninety-four district courts in the federal system, with each state having at least one district. A state with a relatively small population may have only one district. The entire state of South Carolina, for example, makes up the federal District of South Carolina. States with larger populations and higher caseloads are subdivided into more districts. For example, Tennessee has three federal districts: Eastern, Middle, and Western. Mississippi has two federal districts: Northern and Southern.

Intermediate appellate courts in the federal system are called United States Courts of Appeals. There are courts of appeals for each of the thirteen federal circuits. Twelve of these circuits are based on geographic jurisdiction. Eleven numbered circuits cover all the states, and the District of Columbia Circuit is the twelfth geographic federal circuit court of appeals. The thirteenth federal circuit, called the Federal Circuit, hears appeals from district courts in all other circuits on issues related to patent law and from certain specialized courts and agencies.[5] A map showing the federal circuits and underlying districts is available at www.uscourts.gov/images/CircuitMap.pdf. Circuit maps may also be found in the front of the *Federal Supplement* and the *Federal Reporter*, books that publish cases decided by federal courts.

---

5. For more information about this court, see United States Court of Appeals for the Federal Circuit, *About the Court*, http://fedcir.gov/about.html.

Tennessee is in the Sixth Circuit. This means that cases from the Western, Middle, and Eastern District Courts of Tennessee are appealed to the Court of Appeals for the Sixth Circuit. This circuit encompasses Michigan, Ohio, and Kentucky, in addition to Tennessee.

The highest court in the federal system is the United States Supreme Court. It decides cases concerning the United States Constitution and federal statutes. This court does not have the final say on matters of purely state law; that authority rests with the highest court of each state. Parties who wish to have the United States Supreme Court hear their case must file a petition for *certiorari*, as the court has discretion over which cases it hears.

C. Courts of Other States

Most states have the three-tier court system of Tennessee and the federal judiciary, though a few states do not have an intermediate appellate court. Tennessee is one of only four states that have separate courts of appeals to handle criminal and civil matters.[6] Another difference in some court systems is that the "supreme" court is not the highest court. In New York, trial courts are called supreme courts and the highest court is the Court of Appeals. Two other states, Massachusetts and Maine, call their highest court the Supreme Judicial Court.

Citation manuals are good references for learning the names and hierarchies of different court systems, as well as for learning proper citation to legal authorities. The two most popular are *The Bluebook: A Uniform System of Citation*, which is written by students from several law schools,[7] and the *ALWD Citation Manual: A Professional System of Citation*, written by Dean Darby Dickerson and the Associa-

---

6. The other three states are Alabama, Oklahoma, and Texas.
7. *The Bluebook: A Uniform System of Citation* (Columbia Law Review Ass'n et al. eds., 18th ed. 2005). This book's citations conform to the *Bluebook*.

tion of Legal Writing Directors.[8] Appendix 1 of each manual provides information on federal and state courts.

V. Overview of the Research Process

Conducting effective legal research means following a process. This process leads to the authority that controls a legal issue as well as to commentary that may help you analyze new and complex legal matters. The outline in Table 1-2 presents the basic research process.

Table 1-2. Overview of the Research Process

1. Generate a list of *research terms.*

2. Consult *secondary sources* such as practice manuals, treatises, legal encyclopedias, and law review articles. Note new research terms and any citations to primary authorities that appear relevant.

3. Find controlling *constitutional provisions, statutes, court rules,* or *regulations* by reviewing their indexes or searching online databases. Read these authorities carefully, and study the annotations to find cross-references to additional authorities and explanatory materials.

4. Find citations to relevant case law by reading annotations in statutory codes, searching online databases, or using *digests.* A digest is essentially a multi-volume topic index of cases in a certain jurisdiction or subject area.

5. Read the cases fully and carefully, either online or in a *reporter.* A reporter series publishes the full text of cases, in roughly chronological order, in a certain jurisdiction or subject area.

6. *Update* your primary authorities by using a citator such as Shepard's or KeyCite. Updating will let you know whether your authorities are still good law. Updating will also help you find additional relevant authorities.

7. Know you are finished when you *encounter the same authorities* and no new authorities through all the research methods you employ.

---

8. Ass'n of Legal Writing Directors & Darby Dickerson, *ALWD Citation Manual: A Professional System of Citation* (3d ed. 2006).

This basic process should be customized for each research project. Consider whether you need to follow all seven steps, and if so, in what order. If you are unfamiliar with an area of law, you should follow each step in the order indicated, making certain to start with secondary sources. Beginning with secondary sources will provide both context for the issues you must research and citations to relevant primary authority. As you gain experience in researching legal questions, you may choose to modify the process. For example, if you know that a situation is controlled by the common law, you may choose to skip looking for statutes and rules.

A. Generating Research Terms

Many legal resources in print use lengthy indexes as the starting point for finding legal authority. Electronic sources often require the researcher to enter words that are likely to appear in a synopsis or in the full text of relevant documents. To ensure you are thorough in beginning a research project, you will need a comprehensive list of words, terms, and phrases that may lead to law on point. These may be legal terms or common words that describe the client's situation. The items on this list are *research terms.*

Organized brainstorming is the best way to compile a comprehensive list of research terms. Some researchers ask the journalistic questions: Who? What? How? Why? When? Where? Others use a mnemonic device like TARPP, which stands for Things, Actions, Remedies, People, and Places.[9] Whether you use one of these suggestions or develop your own method, generate a broad range of research terms regarding the facts, issues, and desired solutions of your client's situation. Include in the list both specific and general words. Try to think of synonyms and antonyms for each term. Using a legal dictionary or thesaurus may help generate terms.

As an example, assume you are working for a defense attorney who was recently assigned to a burglary case. Around midnight, your

---

9. *See* Roy M. Mersky and Donald J. Dunn, *Fundamentals of Legal Research* 15 (8th ed. 2002) (explaining "TARP," a similar mnemonic device).

client allegedly bent a credit card to spring the lock to a stereo store, where she is accused of having stolen $2,000 worth of equipment. She was charged with first-degree burglary. You have been asked to determine whether there is a good argument for limiting the charge to second-degree burglary based on the fact that she used a credit card and not professional burglar tools. Table 1-3 provides examples of research terms you might use to begin work on this project.

After compiling your initial list of research terms, scan through and pick out the ones that appear most frequently and that you believe are the most important. Use those as your starting point. Remember that as your research progresses, you will learn new research terms to include in the list, and decide to take others off. For example, by reading secondary sources, you may learn a *term of art*, a word or phrase that has special meaning in a particular area of law. Also, remember to return to your list of research terms during your research process in order to refine your research. If you try an online search using words like "burglary," "second degree," and "burglar tools" and get inundated with far too many results, reviewing your

Table 1-3. Generating Research Terms

Journalistic Approach
Who: Thief, robber, burglar What: Burglary, first degree, second degree, crime How: Breaking and entering, burglar tools, trespassing, credit card Why: Theft, stealing, burglary, rob, stolen goods When: Midnight, night Where: Store, building, shop, commercial establishment
TARPP Approach
Things: Burglar tool, credit card Actions: Burglary, breaking and entering, trespassing, crime, using credit card to spring lock Remedies: First degree, second degree People: Burglar, thief, robber Places: Store, building, commercial establishment, business, shop

list of terms to find something more specific, such as "credit card," might help you significantly narrow and focus your potential list of cases to read.

B. Researching the Law — Organization of This Text

The remainder of this book explains how to use your research terms to conduct legal research in a variety of sources. The book begins with primary authority because understanding primary authorities, their structure and organization, is critical to legal research and analysis, and because locating primary authority is the ultimate goal of legal research. Chapter 2 addresses the structure and format of case opinions and reporters, while Chapter 3 is devoted to different ways to research case law by topic. Chapter 4 describes constitutions, statutes, procedural rules, and how to research them, with Chapter 5 giving specific guidance in performing legislative history research. Chapter 6 addresses administrative law. After this focus on finding primary authority, the following chapters explain how and why to update primary authority using citators such as Shepard's and KeyCite (Chapter 7) and how to use secondary sources (Chapter 8). Although secondary sources are covered later in the book, it's important to keep in mind that legal researchers often actually begin their research with secondary materials, especially when researching new or complex areas of law.

Although each chapter includes relevant website addresses for online research, Chapter 9 is focused on how to conduct efficient and effective online research. Although the chapters focusing more on printed materials come earlier in the book, some research projects or classes may require online sources to be used simultaneously with print sources or even before them.

Generally, understanding how print sources are organized and produced leads to better electronic research, as many electronic products are based conceptually on the print versions of the same materials. Legal researchers should be well versed in both print and online sources, as access to both types of sources varies widely, depending on the type of practice one is in or the size of the office. A fluent, effective legal researcher will be able to confidently research using a combination of print materials, various commercial databases, and free Internet sources, and will be able to adapt quickly to new situations and new requirements.

Throughout the book, when a researcher may benefit from knowing exactly which online source contains material covered in a chapter, references to specific Westlaw "databases" and LexisNexis "sources" are provided. These Westlaw databases and LexisNexis sources are subdivisions of the enormous volume of documents available on those services, and they can be accessed with specific codes. On Westlaw, an introductory shortcut screen allows a researcher to enter a "database identifier" at the prompt "Search these databases." For example, TN-CS is the identifier for a database containing cases from Tennessee's state courts. LexisNexis "sources" can be accessed by clicking through directory links or searching the "Find a Source" feature. References to specific Westlaw databases and directions for accessing LexisNexis sources are found throughout this book.

Chapter 10 discusses research strategies as well as how to organize your research. You may prefer to skim that chapter now and refer to it frequently, even though a number of references in it may not become clear until you are more acquainted with legal research resources and their use.

Appendix A provides a summary to finding Tennessee law in print and online. Appendix B contains a selected bibliography of texts on legal research and analysis. The general research texts tend to concentrate on federal sources, supplementing this book's brief introduction to those resources.

Chapter 2

Judicial Opinions and Reporters

A judicial opinion, also informally called a case, is written by a court to explain its decision in a particular dispute. Cases are published in rough chronological order in books called *reporters*.[1] Some reporters include only cases decided by a certain court, for example, the Virginia Court of Appeals, or a system of courts, for example, all Tennessee state courts. Other reporters include cases from courts within a specific geographic region, such as the south-central United States. Still other reporters publish only those cases that deal with a particular topic, such as bankruptcy, education, or rules of civil and criminal procedure.[2] Reporters that publish cases from a particular court or geographic area are the most commonly used by most lawyers and are the focus of this chapter.

I. Reporters for Tennessee Cases

Since 1972, all cases decided with opinions designated for publication by Tennessee appellate courts have been published in the *South Western Reporter*.[3] The *South Western Reporter* also includes opinions from Arkansas, Kentucky, Missouri, and Texas. Table 2-1 gives a quick guide to decoding citations to the *South Western Reporter*. Many

---

1. Digests, books that index and summarize cases by topic, are covered in Chapter 3.

2. Some of these topical reporters are discussed in Part III of this chapter.

3. *See* 230 Tenn., at vi, 496 S.W.2d, at vi (1972) (ordering publication in the *South Western Reporter*).

Table 2-1. Quick Guide to Decoding Citations to the
South Western Reporter

Presley v. Memphis, 769 S.W.2d 221 (Tenn. 1988).

The abbreviation for the *South Western Reporter* is "S.W." This opinion can be found in volume 769 of the *South Western Reporter, Second Series*, starting on page 221.

The case was decided in 1988. The "Tenn." designation informs the reader that this is a Tennessee case, rather than one from Texas or another state whose opinions are included in the *South Western Reporter.*

NOTE: Sometimes when a reporter reaches a certain volume number, the publisher begins another *series.* In 1927, after the publication of volume 300 of the first series, the publisher decided to begin again with volume 1 of the second series. The *South Western Reporter* is currently in the third series.

Tennessee attorneys subscribe to *Tennessee Decisions,* which reprints the Tennessee opinions from the *South Western Reporter* without the opinions from the other states.

These citations to reporters are also used for retrieving cases from online databases such as Westlaw and LexisNexis. Typing "769 SW2d 221" into the "Find" box on Westlaw or the "Get a Document" box on LexisNexis will retrieve the full text of the *Presley v. Memphis* opinion.

Tennessee case opinions included in the *South Western Reporter* are from the Tennessee Supreme Court, the Tennessee Court of Appeals (the civil intermediate appellate court), and the Tennessee Court of Criminal Appeals. Prior to 1972, Tennessee case opinions were also found in reporters published by the state government. Tennessee Supreme Court opinions were published in the *Tennessee Reports* (abbreviated Tenn.), Court of Appeals opinions in the *Tennessee Appeals Reports* (abbreviated Tenn. App.), and Court of Criminal Appeals opinions in the *Tennessee Criminal Appeals Reports* (abbreviated Tenn. Crim. App.).

To further complicate matters, many early volumes of the *Tennessee Reports* are commonly referred to and cited by the name of the person who held the title of "court reporter." For example, the case *Allison v. Allison* may be cited as 9 Tenn. (1 Yer.) 16 (1820). This means that the case can be found at volume 9, page 16 of the *Tennessee Reports*, which is also the first volume of *Tennessee Reports* published by Mr. Yerger, the court reporter. In some instances, the citation may be given as *Allison v. Allison*, 9 Yer. 16 (Tenn. 1860). The easiest way to decipher old citation formats involving the names of court reporters is to compare them against Table T.1 of *The Bluebook: A Uniform System of Citation*, which includes a list of all Tennessee Supreme Court reporters and the abbreviations associated with them.

Other older reporter series for Tennessee are Shannon's *Tennessee Cases with Notes and Annotations* (a three-volume set of edited, annotated, and otherwise unpublished Supreme Court cases from the 1870's through the 1890's), *Tennessee Chancery Appeals Reports* and *Tennessee Chancery Appeals Decisions* (a collection of the opinions of the Court of Chancery Appeals, in existence from 1895–1907),[4] and the *Tennessee Court of Civil Appeals Reports* (containing leading cases from the Court of Civil Appeals from 1909–1919). This last reporter is also occasionally referred to as *Higgins Reports*, in honor of the justice who edited and published the reporter.

While virtually all of the Tennessee Supreme Court's opinions are officially published in the *South Western Reporter*, only about ten percent of case opinions from the intermediate appellate courts are officially published. Unpublished decisions are not binding authority; however, they are considered persuasive authority and in most instances in Tennessee it is permissible to cite to them.[5] Citing to a published decision, though, is always preferable. Although these unpublished decisions are not included in the *South Western Reporter*, they may be available from several other sources. Both published and unpublished case opinions from the past two years may be found on

---

4. Tennessee is one of the few remaining states with a separate set of equity courts, called Chancery Courts. Today, appeals from Chancery Courts go to the Tennessee Court of Appeals rather than to a separate court for chancery appeals.

5. Tenn. Sup. Ct. R. 4(H)(1) (2006). However, this rule is not true in all states. In some states it is not permissible to cite unpublished authority. It is important to know the rule on this issue in the jurisdiction you are writing for.

the web page of the Tennessee Administrative Office of the Courts.[6] Unpublished case opinions are also collected and included in Tennessee case law databases by both LexisNexis and Westlaw (covered in more detail in Chapter 9). They may also be retrieved using commercial document delivery services. The most popular commercial service for obtaining unpublished case opinions in Tennessee is the *Tennessee Attorneys Memo*, discussed in more detail later in this chapter.

Some unpublished cases are further designated "Not for Citation." These cases may not be cited by judges in their opinions, or by litigants in their briefs, except in certain limited circumstances (such as when the opinion is the basis for a claim of *res judicata*).[7]

Cases from state trial courts in Tennessee are not published; in fact, few states publish opinions at the trial court level. Unpublished opinions may be obtained directly from the court that decided the case, and some are available from online services or the *Tennessee Attorneys Memo*.

A. The Anatomy of a Reported Case

A case decision printed in a reporter contains the exact language of the court's opinion. Additionally, the publisher includes supplemental information intended to aid researchers in learning about the case, locating relevant parts of the case, and finding similar cases. Some of these research aids are gleaned from the court record of the case, while others are written by the publisher's editorial staff. This discussion explains the information and enhancements included in the *South Western Reporter*. Most reporters will include most of these items, though perhaps in a different order. Other reporters published by West, in particular, will have nearly identical publisher enhancements and information. To best understand the following discussion, select a volume of the *South Western Reporter* or the *Tennessee Decisions* from the library shelves. Alternatively, refer to the case excerpt in Table 2-2 for examples of the concepts explained below.

---

6. The address is www.tsc.state.tn.us.
7. Tenn. Sup. Ct. R. 4(F)(1), (2) (2006).

Table 2-2. Opening Page from *Woodroof v. Fisher*, 180 S.W.3d 542 (Tenn. Ct. App. 2005)

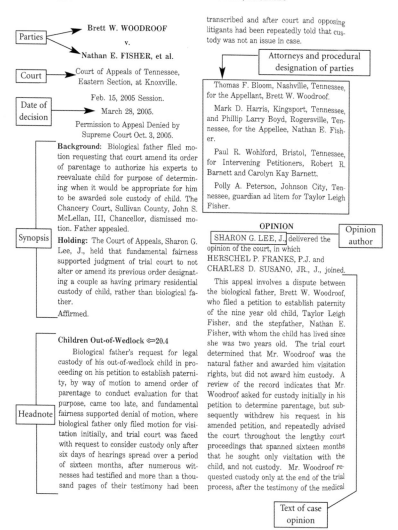

542 Tenn.   180 SOUTH WESTERN REPORTER, 3d SERIES

Parties

Brett W. WOODROOF

v.

Nathan E. FISHER, et al.

Court

Court of Appeals of Tennessee, Eastern Section, at Knoxville.

Feb. 15, 2005 Session.

Date of decision

March 28, 2005.

Permission to Appeal Denied by Supreme Court Oct. 3, 2005.

Background: Biological father filed motion requesting that court amend its order of parentage to authorize his experts to reevaluate child for purpose of determining when it would be appropriate for him to be awarded sole custody of child. The Chancery Court, Sullivan County, John S. McLellan, III, Chancellor, dismissed motion. Father appealed.

Synopsis

Holding: The Court of Appeals, Sharon G. Lee, J., held that fundamental fairness supported judgment of trial court to not alter or amend its previous order designating a couple as having primary residential custody of child, rather than biological father.

Affirmed.

Children Out-of-Wedlock ⟐20.4

Biological father's request for legal custody of his out-of-wedlock child in proceeding on his petition to establish paternity, by way of motion to amend order of parentage to conduct evaluation for that purpose, came too late, and fundamental fairness supported denial of motion, where biological father only filed motion for visitation initially, and trial court was faced with request to consider custody only after six days of hearings spread over a period of sixteen months, after numerous witnesses had testified and more than a thousand pages of their testimony had been

Headnote

transcribed and after court and opposing litigants had been repeatedly told that custody was not an issue in case.

Attorneys and procedural designation of parties

Thomas F. Bloom, Nashville, Tennessee, for the Appellant, Brett W. Woodroof.

Mark D. Harris, Kingsport, Tennessee, and Phillip Larry Boyd, Rogersville, Tennessee, for the Appellee, Nathan E. Fisher.

Paul R. Wohlford, Bristol, Tennessee, for Intervening Petitioners, Robert R. Barnett and Carolyn Kay Barnett.

Polly A. Peterson, Johnson City, Tennessee, guardian ad litem for Taylor Leigh Fisher.

OPINION

SHARON G. LEE, J. delivered the opinion of the court, in which HERSCHEL P. FRANKS, P.J. and CHARLES D. SUSANO, JR., J., joined.

Opinion author

This appeal involves a dispute between the biological father, Brett W. Woodroof, who filed a petition to establish paternity of the nine year old child, Taylor Leigh Fisher, and the stepfather, Nathan E. Fisher, with whom the child has lived since she was two years old. The trial court determined that Mr. Woodroof was the natural father and awarded him visitation rights, but did not award him custody. A review of the record indicates that Mr. Woodroof asked for custody initially in his petition to determine parentage, but subsequently withdrew his request in his amended petition, and repeatedly advised the court throughout the lengthy court proceedings that spanned sixteen months that he sought only visitation with the child, and not custody. Mr. Woodroof requested custody only at the end of the trial process, after the testimony of the medical

Text of case opinion

Source: *South Western Reporter.* Reprinted with permission of West, a Thomson business.

Parties and procedural designations. All of the parties are listed with their procedural designations.[8] In general, if a losing party files an appeal, she will be called the *appellant* and the opposing party will be called the *appellee.*[9] The traditional form in Tennessee calls for parties in civil cases to be designated by their procedural status both at the trial level and at the appellate level. A defendant who lost her case at trial and then appealed would be noted as "Defendant-Appellant."

Court. Immediately after the listing of parties, the court that decided the case will be listed. In most other states, and in older Tennessee cases, the *docket number* will also be included. The docket number is a record-keeping number assigned to the case by the court and is unique to that case—rather like a Social Security number for a case. While the docket number is no longer included in the official publication of the *South Western Reporter,* you will still see it when researching case law online using a service such as Westlaw or LexisNexis.

Dates. Each case will include the date of the court's decision. Some cases may also include the date that the case was argued and submitted to the court, or a date that a higher appellate court denied further review or hearing. For citation purposes, usually only the year that the case was decided is necessary.

Synopsis. One of the most helpful research aids added by the publisher is a synopsis. This is a short summary of the key facts, procedure, legal points, and disposition of the case. Reading a synopsis can quickly tell you whether a case is on point. You cannot rely exclusively on a synopsis; at least skim each case to determine whether it is important for your research. Moreover, you must never cite the synopsis, even when it gives an excellent summary of the case. The synopsis was not written by a judge, but by the publisher, and is therefore not authoritative.

Disposition. The disposition of the case is the court's decision to affirm, reverse, remand, or vacate the decision below. If the appellate

---

8. Recently, Tennessee cases have been reported with the procedural designations of the parties noted only in the *Attorneys* section, discussed below.

9. In other jurisdictions, the term *respondent* is used for the appellee in this situation.

court agrees with only part of the lower court's opinion, the appellate court may affirm in part and reverse in part.

Headnotes. A headnote is a sentence or short paragraph that summarizes a single point of law in a case. Most cases will have several headnotes. The text of the headnote may come directly from the text of the opinion, or it may be an editor's paraphrase of the text. But because only the opinion itself is authoritative, do not rely on headnotes when analyzing cases, and do not cite them in legal documents. In West reporters, each headnote will have a *topic,* such as Children Out-of-Wedlock, and a *key number,* such as 20.4. How to use these topics and key numbers to find additional cases on the same subject is discussed in Chapter 3.

At the beginning of each headnote, immediately before the topic and key number, is a number identifying it in sequence with the other headnotes in that case. Within the text of the opinion, the same sequential numbers will appear in bold brackets[10] at the point in the decision supporting the headnote. Thus, if you wanted to quickly find the text of the opinion supporting the second headnote, you could skim through the case until you located the bold, bracketed [2] in the decision.

Headnotes are generally the product of a given reporter's editorial staff, even when the text of the headnote is identical to the language used in the opinion. Thus, in states where case decisions are published in more than one reporter, the number and text of the headnotes will likely differ depending on which reporter is being used.

Attorneys. The attorneys representing each of the parties, the attorneys' law firms, and the cities in which they practice are listed. In recent Tennessee cases, the listing of the attorneys is also where you will find the parties identified with their procedural designation, such as appellant or plaintiff.

Opinion. The text of the opinion is immediately preceded by the name of the judge who wrote the opinion. In some cases, the names of the judges who heard the opinion may be listed, and those who concurred or dissented will be noted. Note that following a judge's

---

10. In some reporters, the numbers are printed in bold but not bracketed.

name may be "C.J." or chief justice (for the Tennessee Supreme Court), "P.J." or presiding judge (for the Tennessee Court of Appeals or Court of Criminal Appeals) or "J." for another judge or justice. Judges sitting by special designation will be listed as "Special Judge."[11]

If the judges who heard the case do not agree on the outcome or the reasons for the outcome, there may be several opinions for the case. The opinion supported by a majority of the judges is the *majority opinion*. An opinion written to agree with the outcome but not the reasoning of the majority is a *concurring opinion*. An opinion written by a judge who disagrees with the outcome supported by the majority opinion is a *dissenting opinion*. While only the majority opinion is binding precedent, the other opinions provide valuable insights and may be cited as persuasive authority. If there is no majority on both the outcome and the reasoning, the case will be decided by whichever opinion garners the most support, which is called a *plurality decision*.[12]

Variations in reported cases. The items included in a case opinion will vary not just from state to state, and publisher to publisher, but also over time. Comparing current Tennessee cases from the *South Western Reporter* with older cases from the *South Western Reporter* will reveal significant differences in how cases look and what information is published with them. Additional parts of case opinions that you may see in other reporters include a *background* section that summarizes the procedural posture of the case, a concise summary of the court's *holdings*, notation of *parallel citations* to reporters from other

---

11. For example, a trial judge or retired appellate judge invited to hear an appeal would sit by special designation.

12. In Tennessee, as in many states, appellate cases are heard by a three-judge *panel* of the full appellate court. In many other states, a party who does not agree with the decision of the appellate panel may ask for a rehearing *en banc*, meaning that all of the judges on that court would rehear the case. Tennessee, however, does not allow for *en banc* rehearings at the intermediate appellate level, and a party who seeks another hearing must petition the state Supreme Court.

publishers, and *library references* that give cross-references to the relevant sections of secondary sources, such as legal encyclopedias or treatises.[13]

B. Tables and Additional Information in Reporters

Each volume of the *South Western Reporter* contains not just case opinions, but other, related information as well. Information provided in table format includes the following:

- A list of current state supreme court and appellate court judges;
- An alphabetical list of cases reported in the reporter volume;
- A list of cases reported in the volume organized by state;
- A list of all statutes cited in the opinions contained in the volume; and
- A list of *words and phrases*.

The *words and phrases* list identifies, in alphabetical order, all legal phrases that have been defined by a case opinion in the volume. At the end of each volume, the Key Number Digest serves as a subject index to the case opinions, and correlates with the West digests discussed in Chapter 3.

South Western Reporter volumes may also include reprints of recently-amended court rules, rules of procedure, and rules of evidence. They also occasionally include biographies of judges or memorial resolutions passed by state judicial conferences upon the death of a judge.

C. Advance Sheets

The bound volumes of reporters can take months to be published. To make cases available sooner, publishers supply subscribers with *advance sheets.* These are softbound booklets, which can be published

---

13. A summary of the law in an encyclopedia or treatise could provide valuable background information and refer to additional cases or statutes that are on point.

much more quickly than hardbound books. Advance sheets for the *Tennessee Decisions* and for the *South Western Reporter* are published every week.

The spine of each booklet is numbered, beginning with the first issue in January. In addition to the sequential numbers beginning every calendar year, the spine includes a parallel reference to the forthcoming hardbound volume and page numbers. The pagination used in the advance sheets is the same as will be used in the hardbound volumes; thus, a cite to the volume and pages where an opinion appears in the advance sheets will be accurate after the case is published in hardbound volumes.

Advance sheets contain more than just cases. Each advance sheet contains the following:

- a table of cases reported;
- "In This Issue," a topical index to the opinions included in the advance sheet;
- "Judicial Highlights," summaries of notable decisions from around the country;
- a list of recent federal cases organized by subject (*Tennessee Decisions* advance sheets include only federal cases originating in Tennessee, while *South Western Reporter* advance sheets have federal cases originating in all states included in the reporter), and
- a Key Number Digest correlating the cases in the advance sheet with the West digest system.

Additionally, advance sheet booklets may include materials of general interest to the legal community, such as newly-promulgated ABA standards or court rules.

D. Other Sources for Finding Tennessee Cases

To provide access to cases even faster than advance sheets can be published, *slip opinions* of published and unpublished opinions are available either from the court that decided the case or online at www.tsc.state.tn.us (use the drop-down box to browse cases by court and date, or use the "site search" feature to search for cases by party name or key word). A slip opinion is the actual document produced by the court, without the editorial enhancements normally added by the publisher. This means that the slip opinion of a published opinion found at the court website will appear different from the printed version in the *South Western Reporter* and the *Tennessee Decisions*. Updating on the state website varies, but is usually done weekly.

Additionally, many Tennessee attorneys subscribe to *Tennessee Attorneys Memo* (often called simply TAM), a weekly newsletter that summarizes Tennessee case law, legislation, and other legal news. TAM includes references to both officially published and unpublished cases. TAM subscribers can order the full text of any case opinion from TAM's Case Copy Service, or access opinions through a private online database, TAM Online. TAM can usually provide a copy of a case opinion, for a fee, via facsimile within hours of the decision's publication.

Both published and unpublished case opinions are collected by the major providers of legal electronic databases, LexisNexis and Westlaw, and are generally available to subscribers within a few days. They may also be collected and made available by other database providers, such as Loislaw (www.loislaw.com) and VersusLaw (www.versuslaw.com). Using these online systems is covered in more depth in Chapter 9.

II. Reporters for Other States

Many other states continue to publish their own case reporters, and whether a lawyer cites to a state reporter or to one of the commercial regional reporters will vary depending on the citation rules of the state where that lawyer is practicing. Georgia, for example, publishes its Supreme Court cases in the *Georgia Reports* and decisions of Georgia intermediate appellate courts in the *Georgia Appeals Reports*. Georgia cases are also published in the *South Eastern Reporter*, a counterpart of the *South Western Reporter*. Other regional reporters are the *Atlantic Reporter*, *North Eastern Reporter*, *North Western Reporter*, *Pacific Reporter*, and *Southern Reporter*.

The coverage of each regional reporter is decided by West, and it does not correspond with the composition of the federal circuits explained in Chapter 1. Because the states were grouped into regions for case-reporting purposes by West in the 1800's, some of the associations can seem counter-intuitive. Most people today would not think of Tennessee as being in the southwest, but Tennessee remains in the *South Western Reporter* because Tennessee was considered to be in the southwest when the reporters were organized. Similarly, cases from Oklahoma can be found in the *Pacific Reporter*, while cases from Nebraska are in the *North Western Reporter*.

When writing a memo or brief, if you are citing a decision from a state with its own government reporter, and if no rule or custom dictates that you must cite to a specific reporter, cite to the reporter that others reading your document are most likely to have. Often that will be the West regional reporter listed above. For example, if you were practicing in Texas and writing a memo about Arkansas law, you would likely cite to the *South Western Reporter* rather than to the *Arkansas Reports*. Similarly, if you were still in Texas, but writing about Tennessee law and citing to a pre-1972 Tennessee case, you would probably choose to cite to the *South Western Reporter* rather than to the *Tennessee Reports*, as your audience would be more likely to have access to the *South Western Reporter*.

EXAMPLE: *Coca-Cola Bottling Co. v. Gill*, 100 S.W.3d 715 (Ark. 2003).
Tripp v. Miller, 105 S.W.3d 804 (Ark. App. 2003).

If you are not sure which reporter your reader may have access to, you may want to include citations to both reporters. Two citations that refer to the same decision in different reporters are called *parallel citations*.

EXAMPLE: *Coca-Cola Bottling Co. v. Gill*, 352 Ark. 240, 100 S.W.3d 715 (2003).
Tripp v. Miller, 82 Ark. App. 236, 105 S.W.3d 804 (2003).

Table 2-3. Reporters for Federal Court Cases

Court	Reporter Name	Abbreviation
U.S. Supreme Court	*United States Reports* (official) *Supreme Court Reporter* *United States Supreme Court Reports, Lawyers' Edition*	U.S. S. Ct. L. Ed. or L. Ed. 2d
U.S. Courts of Appeals	*Federal Reporter*	F. or F.2d or F.3d
U.S. District Courts	*Federal Supplement*	F. Supp. or F. Supp. 2d

III. Reporters for Federal Cases

So far this chapter has dealt with reporters for Tennessee and other states. Part III explains the reporters for cases decided by the federal courts. Table 2-3 lists the federal court reporters, along with their citation abbreviations.

A. United States Supreme Court

Decisions of the United States Supreme Court are reported in the *United States Reports*, which is the official reporter; the *Supreme Court Reporter*, which is a West publication; and the *United States Supreme Court Reports, Lawyers' Edition*, another unofficial publication, frequently referred to simply as "Lawyers' Edition." Although the *United States Reports* is the official reporter, meaning that you should cite it if possible, that series frequently publishes cases several years after they are decided. Even the advance sheets can run a year or more late. Thus, for recent cases, you will often cite the *Supreme Court Reporter*. Another source for finding recent cases from the Supreme Court is *United States Law Week*. This service publishes the full text of cases from the Supreme Court and provides summaries of important decisions of state and federal courts.

There are a number of online sources for Supreme Court opinions. The Court's website at www.supremecourtus.gov includes slip opinions soon after the decisions are rendered, sometimes on the same day the decisions are rendered. An educational site supported by Cornell University also provides decisions quickly. The address is http://supct.law.cornell.edu/supct/index.html.

B. United States Courts of Appeals

Cases decided by the federal intermediate appellate courts are published in the *Federal Reporter*, now in its third series. The abbreviations for these reporters are F., F.2d, and F.3d. Some Court of Appeals cases that were not selected for publication in the *Federal Reporter* may appear in a relatively new reporter series, the *Federal Appendix*. Cases appearing in the *Federal Appendix* are still referred to as unpublished. The precedential weight given to unpublished federal appellate decisions varies depending on the jurisdiction, so be sure that you know the rules with respect to citing unpublished opinions before using them in your legal documents.[14]

Limited access to recent federal intermediate appellate opinions is available on the U.S. Courts website at www.uscourts.gov and the Cornell website at www.law.cornell.edu/federal/opinions.html. Decisions of the federal intermediate appellate courts are generally available more quickly, and in a more comprehensive fashion, from paid database providers such as LexisNexis and Westlaw. Opinions may also be available from the PACER (Public Access to Court Electronic Records) system, a paid subscription service. Check with your firm or law school librarian to learn whether you have access to decisions and other court documents via PACER.

---

14. Keep in mind that some circuits do not permit their unpublished opinions to appear in the *Federal Appendix* at all, so even taking the *Federal Reporter* and the *Federal Appendix* together, there is no reporter set that publishes all federal Court of Appeals opinions.

C. United States District Courts

Selected opinions from the United States District Courts, the federal trial courts, are reported in the *Federal Supplement*, now in its second series. The citation abbreviation for this reporter is F. Supp. or F. Supp. 2d, depending on the series. Some opinions are available on the U.S. Courts and Cornell websites as well, and both published and some unpublished opinions may be included in the Westlaw and LexisNexis databases.

IV. Topical Reporters

Some reporters publish decisions on a particular topic, rather than cases from a specific court or region. For example, the *Federal Rules Decisions* (abbreviated F.R.D.) includes federal trial court opinions that analyze federal rules of civil and criminal procedure. Similarly, the *Bankruptcy Reporter* includes opinions from federal courts on bankruptcy. Both of these reporters are published by West, so they will contain West's editorial enhancements. Other publishers also provide reporters in topical areas. An example is the *Media Law Reporter*, which publishes all opinions of the United States Supreme Court relevant to media law as well as significant opinions of federal and state courts on the topic of media law.

V. Reading and Analyzing Case Opinions

Once you locate a case, you must read it, understand it, and analyze its potential relevance to the problem you are researching. An attorney, judge, or client who has asked you to do the research will not be satisfied if you report back with a stack of cases you have not yet analyzed.

Do not expect reading a case opinion to be easy. Understanding an opinion will take more mental work than you typically dedicate to a few pages of reading. It is perfectly normal for beginning lawyers to read complex decisions at around ten pages per hour. Often this reading is interrupted by referring to a law dictionary to try to understand the terms used. Early efforts will be more productive if you have a basic understanding of civil procedure terms and the fundamental aspects of case analysis, then follow the strategies outlined at the end of this chapter.

A. A Thimbleful of Civil Procedure

Civil litigation begins when the *plaintiff*—the person who believes he or she was harmed—files a complaint against the *defendant.* The *complaint* names the parties to the lawsuit, states the facts giving rise to it, references applicable law, and asks for relief. Courts vary considerably in how much information is required at this stage of litigation. In general, the complaint must be at least specific enough to put the defendant on notice of the legal concerns at issue and to allow her to prepare a defense. In some states (not including Tennessee), a greater level of detail is required.

The defendant has a limited amount of time in which to file a response to this complaint. In Tennessee, the defendant must file a response within thirty days of being served with the complaint.[15] If the defendant does nothing within the prescribed time, the plaintiff can ask the court for a *default judgment,* which would grant the plaintiff the relief sought in the complaint. The most common form of response to the complaint is an *answer.* In the answer, the defendant admits to the parts of the complaint that she knows are true, denies those things she disputes, and asserts no knowledge of other allegations. The defendant will also raise any available affirmative defenses.

Throughout the litigation, parties submit a variety of documents and briefs to the court for its consideration. Some require no action or response from the court, for example, the filing of the complaint. In other instances, a party asks the court to make a decision or take action. An example is a motion for summary judgment, where a

---

15. Tenn. R. Civ. P. 12.01.

party asks the court to decide in that party's favor without the need for a trial.

When the trial judge grants a motion that ends a case, the losing party can appeal. The appealing party is called the *appellant* or *petitioner,* and the opposing party is the *appellee or respondent.*[16] In deciding an appeal from an order granting a motion, the appellate court decides whether the trial judge was correct in issuing the order at that stage of the litigation. If the appellate court finds that the trial judge made no error, it will *affirm.* If not, it will *reverse* the order granting the motion and *remand* the case back to the trial court.

Even at trial, the parties may make motions that can be appealed. For example, during the trial, the plaintiff presents his evidence first. After all of the plaintiff's witnesses have testified, but before the defendant's witnesses are called, the defendant may move for *judgment as a matter of law,* arguing that the plaintiff cannot win based on the evidence presented, and asking for an immediate decision. An order granting that motion could be appealed.

Many reported case decisions are appeals of orders granting motions. These cases apply different standards of review, depending on the motion that is the subject of the appeal. While standards of review are beyond the scope of this book, understanding the procedural posture of the case is crucial to understanding the court's holding. For example, an opinion of an appellate court could hold that the facts submitted in a defendant's motion for summary judgment in a products liability case did not merit granting a summary judgment, and reverse the trial court. This opinion would have little relevance in another products liability case, no matter how factually similar, if the second case has been tried by a jury and a verdict rendered, because the two cases are in different postures and different standards will apply. The relevant rules of civil procedure will guide your analysis. Texts listed in Appendix B of this book contain helpful explanations as well.

---

16. In Tennessee, the terms used by the Courts of Appeals and the state Supreme Court are *appellant* and *appellee.* In many other states, *appellant* and *appellee* are used at the intermediate appellate level, while *petitioner* and *respondent* are reserved for use by the state Supreme Court.

B. Analyzing the Substance of Case Opinions

Early in your career it may be difficult to determine whether a case is relevant to your research problem. If the case concerns the same legally significant facts as your client's situation and the court applies law on point for your problem, then the case is relevant. Legally significant facts are those that affect the court's decision. Some attorneys call these outcome-determinative facts or key facts. Which facts are legally significant depends on the case. The height of the defendant in a contract dispute is unlikely to be legally significant, but that fact may be critical in a criminal case where the only eye witness testified that the thief was about five feet tall.

Rarely will your research reveal a case with facts that are exactly the same as your client's situation. Rather, several cases may involve facts that are similar to your client's situation, but not exactly the same. Your job is to determine whether the facts are similar enough for a court to apply the law in the same way and reach the same outcome. If a court reached a decision favorable to your client, you will highlight the similarities. If, on the other hand, the court reached an unfavorable decision from your client's perspective, you may argue that the case is distinguishable from yours based on its facts or that its reasoning is faulty.[17] You have an ethical duty to ensure that the court knows about a case directly on point, even if the outcome of that case is adverse to your client.

You are also unlikely to find one case that addresses all aspects of your client's situation. Most legal claims have several elements or factors. *Elements* are required parts of a claim while *factors* are important aspects but not necessarily required. For example, in many jurisdictions, the elements of a claim for battery are the following:

- The defendant committed an intentional act that resulted in a harmful or offensive contact with the plaintiff;

---

17. This discussion assumes that you are preparing a pleading to file in court in which you advocate on behalf of your client. While preparing in-office memoranda, it is important to remain as even-handed as possible in your description and analysis of applicable authorities, so that the client and other attorneys working on the case can make the best judgments possible as to likely case outcomes and the best way to proceed.

- The plaintiff did not consent to the contact; and
- The harmful or offensive contact caused injury, damage, loss, or harm to the plaintiff.

If a court decides that one of these three elements is not met, it often will not discuss the others, as without all three required elements present, the case will fail.

In a different type of case, a court may look at a list of factors rather than elements. In most jurisdictions, in a negligence case, a court will look at certain factors to determine whether the defendant has taken an unreasonable risk. These factors include the following:

- The foreseeable probability of the harm or injury occurring;
- The possible magnitude of potential harm or injury;
- The importance or social value of the activity engaged in by the defendant;
- The feasibility of alternative, safer conduct and the relative costs and burdens associated with that conduct; and
- The relative safety of the alternative conduct.[18]

The court may decide that two factors are so overwhelming that others have little impact on the outcome, and thus address those other factors only briefly, if at all. In these circumstances, if the other factors or elements were important to your case, you would have to find additional cases that analyze them.

Once you determine that a case is relevant to some portion of your analysis, you must decide how heavily it will weigh in your analysis. Two important points need to be considered here. One is the concept of binding precedent; the other is the difference between the holding of the case and dicta within that case.

A case opinion that has decided an issue or principle of law is *binding precedent* with respect to later cases presenting the same issues to lower courts in the same jurisdiction.[19] Thus, the courts must follow

---

18. *See McCall v. Wilder*, 913 S.W.2d 150, 153 (Tenn. 1995) (citing Restatement (Second) of Torts, §§ 292, 293 (1964)).

19. *Black's Law Dictionary* 1214, 1215 (Bryan A. Garner ed., 8th ed. 2004).

prior opinions of higher courts in the same jurisdiction, ensuring consistency in the application of the law. When deciding state law issues, the Tennessee Court of Appeals must follow the decisions of the Tennessee Supreme Court, but not those of the courts of any other state, not the decisions of lower courts in Tennessee, not the decisions of any federal court, and not even earlier decisions of the Tennessee Court of Appeals.

The concept of binding precedent is related to the doctrine of *stare decisis,* which means to "stand by things decided."[20] Under the doctrine of *stare decisis,* courts generally follow their own previous decisions instead of re-opening an issue for a possible different outcome. If a court decides not to continue following its earlier opinions, it is usually because of changes in society that have outdated the law of the earlier case, or because a new statute has been enacted that changes the legal landscape.

Courts are required to follow only the *holdings* of prior cases; that is, the courts' ultimate decisions on the matters of law at issue in the cases. Other statements or observations included in the opinion are not binding; they are referred to as *dicta.* For example, a court in a property dispute may hold that the land belongs to X. In reaching that decision, the court may note that had the facts been slightly different, it would have decided the land belonged to Y. That observation is not binding on future courts, though it may be cited as persuasive authority.

Finally, in determining whether an earlier decision is binding precedent for your issue, you must determine whether that earlier decision has been reversed, overruled, or modified in a way that substantially affects the holding in question. To do this, legal researchers use citator services such as Shepard's and KeyCite. Citator services are discussed in depth in Chapter 7.

After finding a number of cases that have similar facts, that discuss the same legal issue, and that are binding on the court that would hear your client's case, the next step is to synthesize the cases in order to state and explain the legal rule. Sometimes a court states the rule fully; if it does not, piece together the information from the relevant

---

20. *Id.* at 1443.

cases to state the rule completely but concisely. Then use the analysis and facts of various cases to explain the law. Decide how the rule applies to the client's facts, and determine your conclusion. Note that this method of synthesis is much more than mere summaries of all the various cases. Legal analysis texts in Appendix B of this book explain synthesis in detail.

C. Strategies for Reading Case Opinions

As you begin reading opinions, the following strategies may help you understand them more quickly and more thoroughly.

- Quickly review the synopsis (and summary of holdings, if available) to determine whether the case seems to be on point. If so, skim the headnotes to find the particular portion of the opinion that is most relevant. Remember that one opinion may discuss several issues of law, only one or two of which may interest you. Go to the portion of the opinion identified by the relevant headnote and decide whether it is important for your project.
- If so, skim the entire decision to get a feeling for what happened and why, focusing on the portion of the opinion identified by the relevant headnote.
- Read the opinion slowly and carefully, giving extra scrutiny to those parts of the opinion that are most plainly relevant to your legal issue.
- At the end of each paragraph or page, consider what you have read. If you cannot summarize it, try reading the material again.
- The next time you read the case, take notes. The notes may be in the form of a formal case brief or they may be scribbles that only you can understand. Regardless of the form, the process of taking notes will help you identify, parse through, and comprehend the essential concepts of the case. In law school, the notes will record your understanding of the case both for class discussion and for the end of the semester when you begin to review for exams. When preparing to write a legal document, the notes will assist you in organizing your analysis into an outline.

- Note that skimming text online or highlighting a printed page is usually not sufficient to achieve thorough comprehension of judicial opinions.

Chapter 3

Researching Judicial Opinions

As noted in the previous chapter, *reporters* contain judicial opinions, organized in rough chronological order. Usually, though, legal researchers are looking for opinions that address a particular set of facts or a certain issue of law, and thus need to research case law by subject. There are many different ways to locate court opinions on a given subject, and the method that works well in one situation might not be effective in another. Some of the possible research techniques include using a digest, searching through applicable secondary authorities to locate citations to case opinions, starting with a known on-point opinion and finding out what other, later opinions have cited it ("updating"), reading the *Tennessee Attorneys Memo*, and searching full-text electronic databases. Because using digests is a task unfamiliar to most novice legal researchers, and because the other research methods are discussed in different chapters of this book, this chapter will focus mainly on digests.

I. The National Digest System

A digest is a multi-volume index in which case summaries, or headnotes, are organized by subject. Under each subject, the digest provides a headnote from each case that addresses that particular subject and a citation to the case. This chapter concentrates on digests published by West because they are the most widely used. Much of the information provided here would apply to any other case digest as well.

Table 3-1. Excerpts from *West's Tennessee Digest 2d*

Tenn. 2001. Doctrine of mutual combat will not compel, as a matter of law, the reduction of second degree murder to voluntary manslaughter; doctrine was abrogated when revised criminal code was adopted in 1989. State v. Williams, 38 S.W.3d 352.	**Tenn. Crim. App. 1995.** Mutual combat is not a statutory defense to second-degree murder. State v. Johnson, 909 S.W.2d 461.

A. State Digests

The scope of most West digests is based on jurisdiction.[1] The current digest used for researching Tennessee law is *West's Tennessee Digest 2d*. It includes headnotes of cases from state and federal courts in Tennessee. Headnotes from cases that originated in Tennessee and were later decided by the Sixth Circuit and the United States Supreme Court are included, too. This digest also includes references to opinions of the Tennessee Attorney General and articles published by Tennessee law reviews. An example of entries in *West's Tennessee Digest 2d* is given in Table 3-1.

All states have their own digests, with the exceptions of Virginia and West Virginia, whose cases are digested together in the *Virginia Digest;* North Dakota and South Dakota, whose cases are digested together in the *Dakota Digest;* and Delaware, Nevada, and Utah, whose decisions are not in any state digest.[2]

---

1. Some digests are limited by topic, such as the *Bankruptcy Digest* and *Military Justice Digest.*

2. Delaware's cases are digested in the *Atlantic Digest*, and Nevada's and Utah's are in the *Pacific Digest.*

B. Regional Digests

Some digests index cases from a number of different jurisdictions. For instance, the *Atlantic Digest* contains headnotes of cases that are reported in the *Atlantic Reporter*, which were decided by many different state courts in the mid-Atlantic region. Just as regional reporters contain opinions only of state courts, regional digests contain references only to state court opinions, and not to federal court opinions. Of the seven regional reporters published by West, four have corresponding regional digests. Those four regional digests are the *Atlantic Digest*, the *North Western Digest*, the *Pacific Digest*, and the *South Eastern Digest*.[3] Tennessee's cases, which are reported in the *South Western Reporter*, are not included in any regional digest.

C. Federal Digests

Another digest, the *Federal Practice Digest*, provides an index to cases decided by federal trial and appellate courts. The full text of those cases is published in the *Federal Rules Decisions*, the *Federal Supplement*, the *Federal Reporter*, the various reporters for the United States Supreme Court cases,[4] and in other reporters for opinions published by federal courts, such as the *Bankruptcy Reporter*.

D. Combined Digests

West also publishes combined digests, which index the decisions of courts from all fifty states and federal courts as well. The *Decen-*

---

3. There also was a *Southern Digest*, but it ceased publication in 1991. If you encounter a *Southern Digest* in a law library, keep in mind that it will not include references to cases decided after 1991.

4. West publishes a digest for United States Supreme Court cases called *United States Supreme Court Digest*. Another digest for these cases is *United States Supreme Court Digest, Lawyers' Edition*. Note that the *Lawyers' Edition* classification scheme is not identical to the West system.

nial Digests start their coverage in 1897. Initially, a new series was issued every ten years, hence the name, *Decennial*. Thus, a researcher looking at case law from 1897 to 1906 would look in the *First Decennial Digest*. A researcher interested in case law from 1907 through 1916 would look in the *Second Decennial Digest*. In 1976, the publishers at West decided to switch to a five-year publishing schedule, so that a researcher interested in case law from 1996 through 2004 would look at both the *Eleventh Decennial Digest, Part 1* and the *Eleventh Decennial Digest, Part 2*. Anyone researching case law across all time periods from 1897[5] to the present[6] would have to conduct research in fourteen different digest sets. Obviously, this procedure is very time-consuming and cumbersome, and most legal researchers use this only as a last resort. You may find the *Decennial Digest* helpful in the following situations:

- Your library does not contain a digest for the jurisdiction whose laws you are researching.
- There is no law on point in your jurisdiction, requiring you to search the laws of other jurisdictions for persuasive authority.

II. Structure of a West Digest

A. Topics and Key Numbers

West's Tennessee Digest 2d, the *Federal Practice Digest*, and other West digests index cases according to the West system of *topics* and *key numbers*. *Topics* are broad subjects of law. Examples of West topics include "Homicide," "Health and Environment," and "Zoning and Planning." The *key number* relates to a subtopic within that area of law. An example of a topic-key number for homicide cases dealing

---

5. Cases prior to 1897 are digested in the *Century Digest*.

6. Cases that have been published after the issuance of the latest edition of the *Decennial Digest* are digested in the *General Digest*. The *General Digest* is non-cumulative, which means reviewing every volume released since the last edition of the *Decennial Digest* in order to be as up-to-date as possible using the digest system.

with the defense of mutual combat is Homicide 784.[7] The key number 784 refers to the subtopic "Mutual or Voluntary Conduct."

"Homicide" is a vast topic, containing over 1,000 key numbers on subtopics covering different degrees of homicide, capacity, intent, defenses, trials, jury instructions, verdicts, and sentencing and punishment. An example of a much shorter topic, "Dead Bodies," includes just a few key numbers on subtopics addressing issues such as the right of disposition and civil liabilities for improper burial.

B. Headnotes

The digest entries under each topic-key number are copies of the headnotes found at the beginning of judicial opinions published in West reporters. West has assigned each headnote a topic and key number. Each case is indexed in the digest under as many topics and key numbers as it has headnotes in the reporter.

The bulk of each headnote entry is a sentence that summarizes the point of law that is the specific subject of the topic and key number assigned to that headnote. Although the language is often an abridgement that closely follows the language used in the actual case opinion, headnotes are not authoritative and should never be cited.

In a digest, headnotes are arranged under each topic and key number according to the court that decided the case. Federal cases are listed first, followed by state court cases. Within the federal and state court systems, cases are listed according to judicial hierarchy: cases from the highest appellate court are listed first, followed by decisions of intermediate appellate courts, and then trial court cases. Cases from each court are indexed in reverse chronological order. This order is helpful because recent cases, which are listed first, are more likely to be pertinent to legal research.

---

7. Some key numbers have parentheses included in them, and some have decimal points. For example, Homicide 989(2) and Constitutional Law 254.1. In general, the parentheses are used for subheadings within a particular key number, while decimals are used to create new key numbers. Moreover, a revised topic outline may omit a key number that is no longer used.

Table 3-2. Court Abbreviations in *West's Tennessee Digest 2d*

C.A. 6 (Tenn. 1983).	A 1983 case that originated in one of the federal district courts in Tennessee and was decided by the Sixth Circuit Court of Appeals.
E.D.Tenn. 1981.	A 1981 case decided by the United States District Court for the Eastern District of Tennessee.
Bkrtcy.M.D.Tenn. 1993	A 1993 case decided by the United States Bankruptcy Court for the Middle District of Tennessee.
Tenn. 2001.	A 2001 case decided by the Tennessee Supreme Court.
Tenn.Ct.App. 1988	A 1988 case decided by the Tennessee Court of Appeals.
Tenn.Crim.App. 1996	A 1996 case decided by the Tennessee Court of Criminal Appeals.
Tenn.Ch.App. 1899	An 1899 case decided by the Tennessee Court of Chancery Appeals.
Tenn.Civ.App. 1916	A 1916 case decided by the Tennessee Court of Civil Appeals.

At the beginning of each headnote is a court abbreviation and date. The abbreviations are explained in tables at the beginning of each digest volume. Some of the court abbreviations used in the *West's Tennessee Digest 2d* headnotes are noted in Table 3-2, in the order in which they would have appeared under a given topic and key number.

At the end of the digest headnote are citations to any statutes that are cited in the case.[8] This information is followed by the case citation and any parallel citations.

---

8. These citations do not usually follow the format set forth in the *Bluebook* or other citation style manuals and should not be relied upon as a correct example of how to construct a statutory citation. Similarly, the structure of court information, as shown in Table 3-2, does not comport with the *Bluebook* and should not be adopted in your own writing.

Although West may have assigned a topic and key number to a particular point of law, a given jurisdiction may not have decided a case on that point. In that instance, no entries will appear under that topic and key number in that jurisdiction's digest. Instead, you will find a note stating, *"for other cases see the Decennial Digests and WESTLAW."* You can then use the topic and key number to find on-point cases in other jurisdictions, which could be used as persuasive authority.

C. Chronological Coverage Within Digests

West's Tennessee Digest 2d is cumulative, including cases from 1791 to the present. It replaced the first edition entirely. Many other digests are not cumulative. For example, the *Federal Practice Digest 4th* includes headnotes of cases published from the mid-1980s through the present. The previous series, *Federal Practice Digest 3d*, included cases from 1975 through the mid-1980s. To do thorough research in the *Federal Practice Digest*, you would likely need to consult more than one series. Consider the period of time that is pertinent for your research, and then check the introductory information at the front of the digest to determine whether the digest covers that period.

III. Using the Digests

There are several approaches for using digests to conduct research. The approach that legal researchers use depends on the information they have when they begin their research and what they need to find.

A. Beginning with the Descriptive Word Index

Most often legal research begins with a fact pattern and a legal issue, but without any cases on point and without knowing which

Table 3-3. Outline for Digest Research with the Descriptive Word Index

1. Develop a list of research terms.

2. Find the research terms in the Descriptive Word Index, which will list topics and key numbers relevant to those terms.

3. Check the pocket part to the Descriptive Word Index for recently-added topics and key numbers that may be relevant to the issue.

4. Review the case summaries for each of those topic and key number combinations in the main digest volumes.

5. Update each topic and key number combination by checking the pocket parts or volume supplements, the cumulative supplementary pamphlets, and the digests contained in the reporter's most recent advance sheets.

6. Read all of the relevant cases that your research reveals.

---

topics and key numbers may be relevant. In these situations, use the Descriptive Word Index to translate research terms into the topics and key numbers used by the digest to index cases relevant to the client's problem. See Table 3-3 for an outline of this process.

1. Develop a List of Research Terms

Follow the TARPP or journalistic brainstorming method from Chapter 1, or use your own approach to generate a list of research terms that describe the situation you are analyzing.

2. Find the Research Terms in the Descriptive Word Index

The Descriptive Word Index is contained in several volumes usually shelved at the end of the digest. When researching with this index, look up each of your research terms and write down the topic and key number for each term you find that looks relevant. Table 3-4 shows an excerpt from the Descriptive Word Index in *West's Tennessee Digest 2d*. Many topics are abbreviated in the Descriptive Word Index. A list of topics and their abbreviations is included at the front of each index volume.

Table 3-4. Sample Index from "Homicide" Digest Topic

HOMICIDE—Cont'd

MERCY killing, excuse or justification,
  Homic ☞ 101

MISFORTUNE. See heading ACCIDENT
  under this heading.

MOTIVE,
  Admissibility of evidence,
    Burglary, **Homic** ☞ **166(10)**
    In general, **Homic** ☞ **166**
    Insurance proceeds, collection of, **Homic**
      ☞ **166(12)**
    Jealousy, **Homic** ☞ **166(9)**
    Marital difficulties or infidelity, **Homic**
      ☞ **166(7, 8)**
    Robbery, **Homic** ☞ **166(10)**
    Unrequited love, **Homic** ☞ **166(9)**
  Necessity of showing motive, **Homic** ☞ **233**
  Sufficiency of evidence, **Homic** ☞ **233**

Source: *West's Tennessee Digest 2d*. Reprinted with permission of West, a
Thomson business.

Be sure to record both the topic and the key number. Many topics
will have the same key numbers (all topics start with key number 1),
so a number alone is not a helpful research tool.

Do not stop looking up research terms after finding just one
index entry listed with a topic and key number. You should move
on to the next step only when you have a list of topics and key numbers.

If you do not find any of your terms in the Descriptive Word
Index, try to brainstorm for additional research terms. If you still cannot find any terms listed in the index, consider moving to a secondary
source, such as a legal encyclopedia or law review article, or consult-

ing an annotated statutory code, and come back to the digests once
you have learned more about your subject.

3. Check the Pocket Part to the Descriptive Word Index

The information included in the hardbound volumes of the Descriptive Word Index will be only as current as their copyright dates.
To include new topics and key numbers without reprinting an entire bound volume, the publisher prints pocket parts. These are additional pages that are inserted in a slot in the back cover of the
bound volume. Pocket parts are printed annually and sent to every-
one who subscribes to the digest. To be thorough, you must search
these pocket parts for each of your research terms and record any
topics and key numbers you find. If the volume has been printed
within the last year, however, it will not have a pocket part for you
to check.

4. Review the Headnotes for Each Topic and Key Number Combination in the Main Volumes of the Digest

Take your list of topics and key numbers to the main digest volumes and find the volume that contains the topic you believe is most
likely to be on point. Note that the spine of each digest volume does
not list all the topics included in that volume, only the first and last
topic for each volume. For example, in the current *West's Tennessee
Digest 2d*, the topic "Homicide" appears in volume 17A. The spine of
that volume lists the topics "Homestead to Implied and Constructive
Contracts," indicating that the volume includes those topics and others that come between them alphabetically.

At the beginning of each topic you will find a list of "Subjects Included" as well as "Subjects Excluded and Covered by Other Topics."
These lists will help you decide whether that topic is likely to index cases
most relevant to your research. The list of excluded topics may contain
references to other relevant topics found elsewhere in the digest.

After these lists is the key number outline of the topic, under the
heading "Analysis." Longer topics will contain a short, summary outline and then a detailed outline. Many topics follow a general litiga-

tion outline, so that elements, defenses, pleadings, and evidence are discussed in that order.

Take a few minutes to skim the Analysis outline to find any additional relevant key numbers. Then turn to each of the relevant key numbers and review the headnotes there. Write down the citation for each case that you decide is pertinent to your research. At this point, the cites that you include in your notes do not have to conform to any system of citation. Recording the last names of both parties, the volume, reporter, and page number will usually be sufficient.

The process of reviewing case summaries and recording possibly relevant case citations can be tedious. But your painstaking review of the digest materials is essential. To analyze your client's situation accurately, you need to read every relevant case. Hurrying through the digest will allow you to end sooner, but the risk of missing references to crucial cases is too high.

However, you may be selective in deciding which cases to read first. Additionally, when a topic and key number combination contains many pages of case summaries, or when you are working under tight deadlines, you may have to be selective in choosing the cases you are able to read. First focus on those cases that are binding authority in your jurisdiction. Within that subset, you will usually want to start with the most recent cases, because the law may have changed over time. Some case summaries include facts, and a case with facts similar to yours should be included in your written analysis of your client's situation. Never disregard a factually similar case simply because the case reaches a result that would be bad for your client. You may either find a way to distinguish that case, or find an alternative legal basis for your claim, but you may not ever ignore authorities unfavorable to your client.

5.   *Update Each Topic and Key Number in Digests and Reporters*

Again, the headnotes indexed in the digest are only as current as the volume's publication date. If you are holding a hardbound volume with a publication date of 1997, that hardbound volume will not contain headnotes from any cases decided after 1997. Updated information is most often provided through pocket parts. If the updated information is too thick to fit into a pocket part, the publisher will instead provide a soft-cover volume of new materials, which will be shelved next to the volume it updates.

These supplements are in turn updated using *cumulative supplementary pamphlets*. These pamphlets contain updates for all topics, so they are usually shelved after all of the hardbound volumes of the digest. The cover of a cumulative supplement will indicate both its publication date and the date of the pocket part it updates. You must check the supplement each time you do research using the digests in order to find the relevant headnotes that occasionally appear there.

Finally, check for pertinent cases published after the release of the cumulative supplement. Take these steps:

i.   Check the "closing table" at the front of the most recent cumulative supplement or pocket part for your digest volume. The closing table will indicate the last volume of the corresponding reporter that is included in the digest. For example, the closing table might state that the digest ends with volume 175 of the *South Western Reporter, Third Series*.

ii. Since the digest closes with volume 175 of the *South Western Reporter, Third Series*, go to volume 176 of the *South Western Reporter, Third Series*. Check the digest sheets contained at the back of that volume to see if any headnotes for your topic and key number are included in that volume.

iii. Repeat the check of digest pages for each individual volume of the *South Western Reporter, Third Series*, from volume 177 through the most recent volume and advance sheets on your library's shelves.

You may rarely find your topic included in the digests of the recent reporter volumes, but you cannot ignore the possibility of a highly-relevant case lurking in those recent volumes. Of course, there will always be some window of time between when a court releases its opinion, the publication of that opinion in paper format, and when those paper volumes actually reach the library and are placed on the shelves. To be as current as possible, you must go to an online database, such as LexisNexis or Westlaw.[9]

6. *Read the Relevant Cases that Your Research Reveals*

You must read the relevant cases that you found using the digests. In fact, unless you have specific instructions to provide only a list of cases that may be relevant, your primary task will be to analyze the cases and apply them to your client's situation. Review Chapter 2, Part V on analyzing individual cases.

Reading the cases and understanding the law will be easier if you organize your approach. First, review your list of all the cases that you found. You may notice some cases appear twice because they were indexed under several topics and key numbers. Strike out the duplicates. Next, organize groups of cases according to jurisdiction and then by decision date. While learning how the law developed over time in each jurisdiction will be easier if you read the cases starting with the earliest and moving to the most recent, finding the current rule of law will likely be easier if you begin with the most recent cases. Define your goal and organize the order in which you read the cases accordingly.

Next, go to the reporters and find each case you have listed. Quickly skim the case, paying particular attention to the synopsis and the portions of the case on which the most relevant headnotes were based. Only when you have completed this process should you consider photocopying, printing, or taking extensive notes from it. Do not waste paper, money,[10] or your time by delaying the case analysis portion of your research.

---

9. Note that only Westlaw allows you to continue your research using West topics and key numbers.

10. LexisNexis and Westlaw printing is usually included in law school fees, and thus appears to be free for law students. Printing is generally restricted in the practice of law because it is so expensive. Often print charges are added to a flat fee for unlimited use in contracts that firms have with LexisNexis or Westlaw. Even if those charges are included in the flat fee agreement, lawyers and research clerks will try to limit their printing so that when it comes time to re-negotiate their flat fee arrangement, they can point to their low volume of printing and get the best possible price.

In addition to taking notes on individual cases, pay attention to how the cases fit together. Look for trends in the law and in the facts of the cases. Has the law remained unchanged, or have new elements been introduced? Has the meaning of an important term evolved? Have certain facts virtually guaranteed success for one party, while other facts have tended to cause difficulties? Does one case summarize the current rule, or do you have to synthesize a rule from several cases?

B. Beginning with a Relevant Case

If you begin your research knowing one case on point, you can take a shortcut and bypass the Descriptive Word Index. Read the case in a West reporter and identify the headnotes that are relevant to your issue. Note the topic and key number combinations given for each relevant headnote. Other cases that use these topics and key numbers will likely be helpful to your research and analysis.

Make a list of the relevant topics and key numbers from your case, then go to the main volumes in the digest. Select a volume containing one of the topics on your list. Within that topic, find the key number given in the pertinent headnote. Under the key number, you will see all the headnotes that also have been assigned that same topic and key number. Repeat this step for each relevant topic and key number in your original case. Remember to update your search to find the most recent cases on point.

Occasionally, particularly when you are dealing with an older case as your starting point, you may find that the key numbers within a given topic have changed. For example, your starting case may reference Civil Rights 58—but when you attempt to look up Civil Rights 58 in the applicable digest, you find that topic and key number combination simply doesn't exist, or that it has no connection to the issue you are attempting to research. This situation happens when West has re-ordered a topic, usually to add more key numbers to a topic that is the subject of growing litigation, and may have new elements, new defenses, or entirely new claims. After such a re-ordering, West will place a table at the beginning of the topic. Use that table to translate the old topic and key number to a new topic and key number.

When starting with a known case, you will usually want to expand your research by checking the Analysis at the beginning of the topic to see if there are related key numbers that could contain additional headnotes that would be relevant. Furthermore, you may still need to use the Descriptive Word Index if the case you have at the beginning of your research contains only one topic and key number combination on point. In this situation, check the index to ensure that you have not missed a line of cases that is indexed under another topic and key number.

C. Beginning with the Topic Analysis

After you have researched a specific area of law many times, you may be very familiar with the topics under which cases in that area are indexed. If so, you can begin your research using the Analysis outline that appears at the beginning of each relevant topic. Scan the list of key number subtopics, and then review the headnotes under each key number that appears to be on point. As always, remember to check the pocket parts, supplementary pamphlets, and reporter advance sheets for more recent cases under the topics and key numbers you are searching. Even when beginning research with the topic analysis, it is a good idea to check the Descriptive Word Index at some point for additional material.

D. Beginning with the Words and Phrases Volumes

To learn whether a court has defined a term, refer to the Words and Phrases volumes at the end of the digest.[11] While a dictionary like *Black's Law Dictionary* will provide a general definition of a term, Words and Phrases will direct you to a case that defines a term for a particular jurisdiction. (See Table 3-5.) Judicial definitions are especially helpful when an important term in a statute is vague. For ex-

---

11. Be very careful not to confuse the Words and Phrases volumes with the similarly-named Descriptive Word Index volumes, which are usually shelved immediately adjacent to each other.

Table 3-5. Excerpt from Words and Phrases in *West's Tennessee Digest 2d*

VEHICLE
> Tenn.App. 1963. A sled is a "vehicle" within statute detailing right of way when it is sliding by force of gravity on ice and snow and not being pulled by a person. T.C.A. §§ 59-801, 59-828(b).—Davenport v. Robbins, 370 S.W.2d 929, 51 Tenn. App. 600—Autos 154.

ample, your client might have been charged with driving under the influence when riding a bicycle. The statute on drunk driving might refer to a "vehicle." A judicial opinion defining what constitutes a "vehicle" in your jurisdiction, under your drunk driving statute, would be tremendously helpful.[12]

Note that entries in Words and Phrases refer to cases that provide judicial definitions of terms, while the entries in the main digest volumes, indexed under topics and key numbers, refer to cases that discuss, explain, and possibly define a term. The cases referenced in Words and Phrases are thus a specific subset of the cases that appear under related topics in the main digest volumes. At the end of each entry in the Words and Phrases volumes, West lists the topics and key numbers used for that case's headnotes. The example in Table 3-5 includes the topic and key number Automobiles 154. The information in the Words and Phrases volumes is updated with pocket parts.

E. Beginning with the Table of Cases

The Table of Cases lists all the cases indexed in a particular digest series by both the primary plaintiff's name and the primary defendant's name. This table is helpful when you do not know the citation to a rel-

---

12. West also publishes a much larger set, *Words and Phrases*, containing these judicial definitions from all federal and state jurisdictions combined.

evant case but do know the name of at least one of the parties. The Table of Cases provides the full name of the case, the citation for the case, and the relevant topics and key numbers. After consulting the Table of Cases, you could either read the case in a reporter or continue working in the digest using the topics and key numbers to find more related cases.

Alternatively, if you begin your research with a case that does not include West topics and key numbers, you can use the Table of Cases volumes to learn which topics and key numbers are used for the case's main points of law. For example, if you had a copy of an older Tennessee case from the *Tennessee Appeals Reports*, it would not have West headnotes with topics and key numbers, as that reporter was not published by West. You could look up that case by name in the Table of Cases, and find a parallel citation to the *South Western Reporter* and a reference to the topics and key numbers that West assigned to the case.

IV. Additional Methods of Researching Case Law

Although a digest is a comprehensive and useful tool for locating case law, there are other ways to locate cases that an efficient researcher should consider — particularly when digest research is not proving particularly fruitful. Tactics such as starting with secondary sources, using annotated codes, updating known case law, and searching electronic databases may be more effective than starting with a digest in some situations.

A. Starting with Secondary Sources

When you are researching an area of law or a particular issue that is new to you, starting with a secondary source will often be the best route. When you are new to an area of law, you may not know the terms of art used by lawyers and judges in describing the issues and possible defenses, or you may not even know what those issues and defenses are likely to be. Starting with a secondary source, such as a legal encyclopedia, the *American Law Reports*, a treatise geared towards practitioners, or a law review article, can be of immense help.[13]

A good secondary source will explain this new area of law to you and help you sort out what issues, theories, and defenses you should be focusing on. Moreover, it will provide citations to important cases, statutes, and regulations, and perhaps provide brief summaries of those primary authorities.[14] Of course, simply relying on secondary sources in preparing your legal research is never acceptable. You will always want to read and update[15] the primary authorities you find cited in your secondary sources. Secondary sources should be a starting point for your research and no more.

Another consideration to keep in mind with secondary sources is jurisdiction. The ultimate goal of virtually all legal research is on-point primary authority from the jurisdiction governing the issue being researched. Many secondary sources, however, have a nationwide focus and attempt to describe the law and legal trends from all over the country. Where possible, start with secondary sources that

---

13. What these secondary sources are, and how best to use them, is discussed in depth in Chapter 8.

14. Since most good secondary sources focus on the important cases, using a secondary source helps avoid a pitfall inherent in digest-based research. In a digest, all headnotes to cases are presented in an equal light. While it is possible to pick out the likely relevant cases by looking at which court decided the case, when it was decided, and the text of the headnote, there is no additional information in a digest to guide a researcher to the seminal cases on an issue. Good secondary sources perform this function.

15. Keep in mind that some secondary sources, such as law review articles, are never updated with pocket parts or supplements, while others may be updated in a slower or more haphazard fashion than digests or annotated codes. A law review article published ten years ago might espouse a theory long-since considered and disregarded by courts and legislatures, and the cases it cites all may have been overruled.

focus exclusively on your jurisdiction, such as your state's legal encyclopedia, or a law review article describing trends in your federal circuit.

B. Starting with an Annotated Code

When your research issue turns on interpretation or application of a statutory provision, consulting an annotated code should almost always be your first choice. Annotated codes provide both the language of the statutes and references to cases that interpret and apply the statutes. For instance, you could be representing a defendant in a lawsuit in Knox County. Based on some of the facts your client told you, you believe that venue would more appropriately lie in neighboring Blount County. You are considering taking a wait-and-see approach, and deciding whether to petition to move the case to Blount County in several weeks, after you get a feel for whether the Knox County judicial system might be in some way better for your client and the case.

At this point, you would need to research whether there is a requirement that you file the petition immediately. In litigation, parties are often required by statute or rule to exercise their rights immediately or risk losing those rights. Since procedures and requisites for filing a change of venue are ordinarily statute-based or rule-based, your first step would be to turn to the *Tennessee Code Annotated* to locate applicable statutes on venue. You would find Tenn. Code. Ann. §20-4-201, which specifies when venue is changeable. However, the statute itself is not specific as to when the petition must be filed—only that it may be filed any time before trial. Perhaps a case exists that sheds more light on how this statute has been interpreted and enforced.

Instead of looking for case law using the digests or secondary sources, your next step should be to skim the "Notes to Decisions"— summaries of judicial opinions that relate to that statute. The Notes to Decisions are organized by topic, so that the researcher can quickly find those cases touching on a particular issue. In those Notes, you will find the following under the heading "Time for Filing Petition."

> Ordinarily there is no particular set time that a petition for change of venue should be filed. It should, though, be filed at the first opportunity after knowledge of the facts upon which the petition is based come to those filing such petition. *Tennessee Gas Transmission Co. v. Oakley*, 193 Tenn. 638, 249 S.W.2d 880 (1952).[16]

This case looks like a promising start. Your next step would be to read the full text of the case. From there, you could note the applicable topics and key numbers and look them up in *West's Tennessee Digest 2d* to find out if there are more cases on this issue, or you could go straight to a citator service (such as Shepard's or KeyCite, discussed in Chapter 7) to see if there are more cases on point.

C. Starting with a Known Case and Updating It

As mentioned above in Part III B, if you start with a known case, you can use the topics and key numbers from that case to find more cases on the same point using the digest system. Another way to use a known relevant case is to update it: use the Shepard's service on LexisNexis or the KeyCite service on Westlaw. Although these systems have noteworthy differences, they perform essentially the same function. A researcher enters a citation[17] into the database, and receives an on-screen report listing other cases that have cited the initial case. The report also lists secondary sources, such as law review articles, that have cited the case.

A judge who writes an opinion in one case usually cites to an earlier case because that earlier case has significant similarities to the current case, either in fact, in law, or in both. Thus, using an updating service not only tells you whether your case has been overruled, reversed, or criticized, but also helps you find later cases that treat your

---

16. Tenn. Code Ann. § 20-4-201 (1994), n. 2.

17. Ordinarily, Shepard's and KeyCite are used for updating case law, but they can be used to update statutes, federal regulations, and some secondary sources as well.

initial case positively, and which may be even more on-point for your own situation that you are researching. Both Shepard's and KeyCite have features that allow you to customize the report you receive. For example, if you want to see only later cases that address one particular point of law in the initial case, and only from your jurisdiction, you can use the customizing options to do so.

D. Searching Electronic Databases

Searching electronic databases of case law, such as those found on Westlaw and LexisNexis, can be an efficient and effective method to find on-point decisions. Sometimes, though, online searching is time consuming and fruitless. Before jumping online and starting your search, use the TARPP or journalistic method to construct a list of search terms. Consider it carefully. Are the terms in your list broad, frequently-used, and apt to be found in case opinions on issues other than your specific issue? If so, stay away from computers and turn instead to digests, annotated codes, or secondary sources. Computer searching will likely lead to unwieldy lists of numerous case citations. Relevant cases may be sprinkled throughout, but not easily identifiable. If your terms are narrow, precise, and likely to be found only in those case opinions that really do address your question, LexisNexis or Westlaw may be your best option. In this situation you are likely to retrieve a manageable list of cases that you can easily skim through to assess the relevance of your results.

As an illustration, imagine researching two different questions. The first question is how notice must be published when a deed of trust is being foreclosed upon. The search terms you decide are most applicable are: notice, publication, deed of trust, and foreclosure. Your second question is what a fertility clinic should do when the frozen embryos being stored there by a once-married couple become the subject of a dispute in a divorce. The search terms you come up with are: fertility, infertility, embryo, frozen embryo, fetus, husband, wife, and divorce.

Running these terms through the Tennessee case law database on Westlaw produces very different results, as shown in Table 3-6. The

Table 3-6. Electronic Search Results

Search Terms	Number of Cases Retrieved
Notice and publ! and "deed of trust" and foreclos!	200
Clinic and embryo and husband and wife	4

foreclosure search retrieves 200 cases while the embryo search retrieves four.

Although you might initially be inclined to think that two hundred possibly on-point cases is a better result than four possibly on-point cases, keep in mind that you must at least skim each case to determine whether it is relevant or not. Your result list of two hundred cases could keep you busy researching for several days what is really a straightforward issue. In contrast, you could easily find an initial answer to this question, and summaries of cases organized by topic, by looking in the index to the *Tennessee Code Annotated* under "Foreclosure-Notice." This research would take about five minutes.

Chapter 4

Constitutions, Statutes, and Procedural and Ethical Rules

I. Constitutions

A *constitution* is the fundamental governing document of a state. It spells out the rights, duties, and powers of the various branches of government, and typically cannot be amended by the legislature alone.

A. The Tennessee Constitution

The first Tennessee constitution was adopted in 1796. This constitution, largely modeled on the constitution of neighboring North Carolina, was in many ways remarkably democratic, and was described by Thomas Jefferson as "the least imperfect and most republican of the state constitutions." It allowed the vote to all free men over the age of twenty-one, regardless of race or property ownership. The governor was to be directly elected, rather than selected by the legislature. Voting, in a striking change from practices followed elsewhere, was to be conducted by secret ballot.[1]

However, there were problems with the first constitution. One of the primary criticisms was that the legislature was given too much

---

1. Lewis Laska, *The Tennessee State Constitution: A Reference Guide*, 2–7 (1990) (quoting Ramsey, *The Annals of Tennessee to the End of the Eighteenth Century*).

power, and the governor, too little. A constitutional convention was called in 1834, and a new constitution was ratified in 1835. The major changes emerging with the new constitution included strengthening the executive and judicial branches, changes to taxation, and, in a major step backwards, reserving the power to vote to white men only. The full text of the Constitutions of 1796 and 1835 are set out in an appendix at the end of Volume 1 of the *Tennessee Code Annotated.*

After the Civil War and following four years of state government controlled by Union sympathizers, a constitutional convention was held in 1870. A new constitution was ratified in 1870, and the Constitution of 1870 remains the basis for the current constitution. Most of the changes to the constitution adopted in 1870 were made in response to what were seen as excesses and corrupt practices by Governor William ("Parson") Brownlow and the Unionist government. The right of suffrage was expanded and the powers of the Governor greatly diminished.[2]

The Tennessee Constitution has been amended several times since 1870. Some of the changes were brought about via constitutional conventions (in 1953, 1959, 1965, 1972, and 1977), and others via a legislation-and-referendum method. These amendments dealt with issues as weighty as school segregation and as seemingly trivial as the term of office for trustees.

In many respects, the provisions of the Tennessee Constitution parallel those of the United States Constitution. Article I of Tennessee's constitution ensures religious liberty, freedom of the press, the right to a jury trial, and the right to be free from unreasonable searches and seizures. Articles II through VII delineate the powers of the various branches and departments of government.

However, like many other state constitutions, the Tennessee Constitution also covers some matters often thought of as being more

---

2. In the aftermath of the Civil War, the right to vote had been stripped from Confederate sympathizers. The 1870 Constitutional Convention restored the vote to the former rebels and their allies. The Constitution of 1870 also severely limited the power of the governor to use the state militia. Laska, *The Tennessee State Constitution*, at 14–17. Governor Brownlow had used the state militia to attempt to halt the predations of the newly-formed Ku Klux Klan.

statutory in nature. For example, Article II, Section 33 prohibits the issuance of state bonds to railroads that are in default in paying interest on earlier state bonds.

B. Researching the Tennessee Constitution

The Tennessee Constitution is published, together with annotations, in the first volume of the *Tennessee Code Annotated*, immediately following the United States Constitution.[3] A separate index to the Tennessee Constitution is included in the back of Volume 1 of the *Tennessee Code Annotated*. This set also has a multi-volume general index, shelved at the end of the set, that provides references to both constitutions and to statutes.

As explained in Chapter 1, begin constitutional research by generating a list of research terms from the facts and issues of your problem. Search the indexes for terms and record the references given. For example, the general index contains under the term "Searches and Seizures" references to Article I, Section 7 of the Tennessee Constitution and to many related statutes.

Once you find a provision of the Tennessee Constitution that applies to your problem, check the annotations that follow immediately after it. Cases that have interpreted that part of the Constitution will be summarized and cited. If there are numerous cases that have discussed a particular section, their summaries will be organized by topic, with a table of contents provided at the beginning. The annotations may also provide historical notes and citations to law review articles, treatises, and opinions of the Tennessee Attorney General, all of which may be helpful in learning about a particular constitutional provision. Be sure to check any pocket parts or free-standing supplements for the most recent amendments to the Constitution as well as new cases and interpretative materials.

Resources available for researching Tennessee constitutional conventions will vary depending on the convention. More recent consti-

---

3. It is also published in the first two volumes of *West's Tennessee Code Annotated*, an unofficial publication of Tennessee's statutes and constitution.

tutional conventions, such as those of 1977 and 1965, were recorded in detail, and all of the debates and documents were published in indexed, bound volumes, such as the *Journal of the Debates of the Constitutional Convention of the State of Tennessee* (1977). Earlier conventions were not as well documented, but journals and papers do exist. The *Journal of the Proceedings of the Convention of Delegates Elected by the People of Tennessee* documents the 1870 constitutional convention, while the *State of Tennessee Constitutional Convention of 1959*, of course, documents that of 1959. However, access to these documents may be limited. Other possible sources to find journals and proceedings for early Tennessee constitutional conventions include microfiche sets such as CIS's *State Constitutional Conventions* or paid subscription databases such as *The Making of Modern Law*. Check with a librarian at your library for access to such services.

C. Researching the Federal Constitution

The United States Constitution is published as part of the sets the *United States Code*, the *United States Code Service*, and the *United States Code Annotated*, which are discussed in more detail in Part II of this chapter. Just as with researching the Tennessee Constitution, the first step is usually to find an index to the Constitution, then to read any applicable provisions, and to find judicial decisions interpreting and applying the constitution.

II. Statutes

Statutes could affect almost every legal issue you deal with in practice. Because law students, particularly early in their law school careers, spend tremendous amounts of time and energy focused on reading and interpreting case opinions, they often receive an impression that judicial authorities are what they will spend the vast majority of their professional lives researching. Many are surprised to find later that statutes, rather than cases, will be the primary focus of much or even most of their professional research and analysis.

Statutes may address substantive issues, such as whether someone who serves alcohol to another who is obviously already drunk can be held liable for any injuries that result from an accident involving the drunk individual. Statutes can also affect related, procedural issues, such as a statute of limitations, which sets the amount of time a potential litigant has to file a lawsuit. Areas of law that have developed recently, such as the use of electronic signatures, or software licensing, will typically be governed by statutes.

A. Publication of Statutes

When a law is first enacted, it is published in an individual format called a *slip law*. The name "slip law" derives from the traditional publication of statutes on individual slips of paper, rather than being bound into a book with other statutes. Recently, though, some states have done away almost entirely with distribution of slip laws in paper and now publish them only in electronic format. Tennessee is one of those states.[4] Researchers looking for recent Tennessee legislation will find it online at http://tennessee.gov/sos/acts/index.htm. The acts are searchable by key word and indexed by legislative session.

After the conclusion of each legislative session, all the laws passed in that session are published in the *Public and Private Acts of the State of Tennessee*, which is also referred to as the Tennessee session laws. *Session laws* is a generic term for a series in which all the laws passed by a legislature in a legislative session are published, with the laws arranged chronologically.

The laws passed by the legislature and signed by the Governor are then *codified*, meaning that they are integrated into the *Tennessee Code Annotated*, which contains all laws currently in effect in Tennessee, arranged by subject. The *Tennessee Code Annotated* is di-

---

4. Tenn. Code. Ann. § 12-6-116 (1999).

vided into seventy-one *titles*, each on a particular subject. For example, Title 36 contains domestic relations laws, and Title 68 consists of laws on health, safety, and the environment. Each title is further subdivided into *chapters* that address particular topics in each subject area, and each chapter is broken down into individual *sections*. Within Title 36, Chapter 1 deals with adoption, and Section 119 of that chapter addresses the filing of a final order of adoption. A citation to that particular law reads: Tenn. Code Ann. §36-1-119.

There are two versions of the *Tennessee Code Annotated* currently published in print and online. The official print version is published by LexisNexis, and it should be the version to which you cite if at all possible.[5] West also publishes an unofficial version of the *Tennessee Code Annotated* both online and in print. The text of the statutes themselves, as well as their arrangement and numbering, will be the same in each set of books. The editorial enhancements added by the publisher, such as indices and references to case opinions, may vary.

B. Researching Statutes in the *Tennessee Code Annotated*

There are a number of different approaches to finding statutes that bear on a research issue. Table 4-1 outlines the basic process. The most efficient approach will vary depending on the issue you are researching and the other resources you have available. It is important to be flexible in your research and recognize that if one approach is not working, you may want to rethink your strategy and try a different method. Whichever method you choose, make sure that you start with an expansive list of research terms by brainstorming using the journalistic or TARPP method from Chapter 1.

---

5. While LexisNexis's online *Tennessee Code Annotated* corresponds with its print version, you should cite to the official print version rather than the online version.

Table 4-1. Outline for Tennessee Statutory Research

1. Generate a comprehensive list of search terms.

2. Look up those search terms in the index to the *Tennessee Code Annotated* to find references to relevant statutes. Alternatively, browse the tables of contents in the relevant code titles, read pertinent secondary sources to find citations to the statutory code, or use the search terms to search an online database of the *Tennessee Code Annotated*.

3. Locate, read, and analyze the potentially relevant statutes in the *Tennessee Code Annotated*.

4. Refer to the annotations following the text of any relevant statutes to find citations to related statutes, cases that interpret the statutes, and additional explanatory materials.

5. Read and analyze the materials found in Step 4.

1. Finding Relevant Statutes

a. Researching Code Books — Starting with the Index

Often the fastest way to do statutory research is to start with the index volumes that you will find at the end of the *Tennessee Code Annotated*. Be careful to look up all of your key words in the index and follow any suggested synonyms or cross-references that you find, rather than just assuming that the first statute you are referred to is the only and best answer. Write down all of the statutory references that you find in the index and make sure to follow up on all of them.

b. Researching Code Books — Using the Tables of Contents

Each title of the *Tennessee Code Annotated* has a table of contents, as does each chapter within each title. If you are confident that you know which title controls your issue, you may start your research by scanning the tables of contents to find the pertinent statutes. Be very careful with this research method, as it can work only if you are correct in your assumption about which title to start with, and making that determination can be problematic even for an experienced researcher. If you are trying to find the statutes related to the crime of driving under the influence of alcohol and spend your time skimming through the tables of contents for Title 39, Criminal Offenses, you will miss the relevant statutes in Title 55, Motor Vehicles.

c. Researching Statutes—Starting with Secondary Sources

In some instances, an efficient way to find controlling statutes is to start with secondary sources. Particularly when you are new to an area of law, a secondary source such as a practitioner's manual can explain the law and put it in context while also providing citations to the controlling statutes. Keep in mind that you would never simply rely on someone else's interpretation of the law, even if that person wrote the most prestigious and well-respected treatise on the subject. You will always want to read the underlying primary authorities, including statutes, for yourself, and make your own conclusions about how they affect your legal research issue.

d. Researching Statutes—Online Sources

The *Tennessee Code Annotated* is available in many electronic versions, including those on Westlaw and LexisNexis. An unannotated version of the code is available for free at www.michie.com as well. Although many novice legal researchers find it difficult to believe, researching statutes by searching an online database of them is hardly ever as fast and reliable as using books. As a general rule, you must be very skilled and experienced in statutory research to anticipate the exact words used by the legislature in drafting a statute. If you do not have those exact words in your search terms online, you will usually perform fruitless searches, wasting money and time. If you do search statutes online, be sure to plan your searches very carefully before signing on. Keep in mind the importance of synonyms, antonyms, spelling variants, and word forms in composing your searches. Composing effective searches online is discussed in more depth in Chapter 9.

2. Reading the Statutory Language

For each statutory citation you found in the index, table of contents, or secondary sources you used as a starting point, select the volume of the *Tennessee Code Annotated* that contains the title of your

Table 4-2. Example Tennessee Statute

Tenn. Code Ann. § 39-14-404. Especially aggravated burglary. — (a) Especially aggravated burglary is:

(1) Burglary of a habitation or building other than a habitation; and

(2) Where the victim suffers serious bodily injury.

(b) For the purpose of this section, "victim" means any person lawfully on the premises.

(c) Especially aggravated burglary is a Class B felony.

(d) Acts which constitute an offense under this section may be prosecuted under this section or any other applicable section, but not both.

[Acts 1989, ch. 591, § 1; 1990, ch. 1030, § 24.]

---

statute[6] and then find the statute itself. When researching online, you will often have to skim through lists of potentially relevant statutes before clicking to a screen that contains the statute itself.

The next step is the most important: *read* the statute very carefully.

Too many researchers fail to take the time necessary to read the language of the statute and consider all its implications before deciding whether it is relevant to the research problem. Further, to understand a single statute you may have to read other, related statutes. For example, one statute may contain general provisions while another contains definitions. Yet another statute may contain exceptions to the general rule. The statute in Table 4-2, Tenn. Code Ann. § 39-14-404, concerns "especially aggravated burglary." To understand the statute, the researcher has to refer to another section, 39-14-402, which provides the definition of burglary, as well as to 39-14-401, which defines terms such as habitation. Section 40-35-111 provides the penalty for committing a Class B Felony.

---

6. Be careful in selecting the code volumes. Each volume has a large number on the spine that designates the volume number in the series, starting with Volume 1 and going through Volume 16. Many of the volumes contain several titles, and the title numbers are also on the spine but in a much smaller print. A common mistake is for someone looking for Title 6 to accidentally pick up Volume 6 instead.

When researching using code books, make sure to check to see if the statute has been amended or repealed.[7] Hardbound code books are initially kept current with a softbound "pocket part" tucked into the back cover of the volume. Pocket parts are published annually. Hardbound code volumes may also be kept current with freestanding softbound supplements that are shelved either next to each hardbound volume, or at the end of the code set. Recent amendments to a law, and information indicating whether a law has been repealed, will be found in these supplemental volumes if a hardbound volume is more than a year old. The new materials in these volumes are organized by statute number, so it is easy to look up a statute and note any changes. If you do not find any reference to the statute in the supplemental materials, the statute was not amended or repealed during the time between publication of the hardbound volume and the supplemental volume or pocket part.

Many researchers will start their research by looking up their statute in the pocket part and freestanding supplements first, so that they do not waste time studying a version of the statute in the hardbound volume that they later discover has been amended or repealed. Regardless of where you start your research, by the time you conclude, you should have checked any available pocket parts and supplements to make sure that you have the most recent version of the statute, as well as references to the most recent case law interpreting the statute.

Since pocket parts are published only annually, there is always a chance that if the legislature is in session, your law has been amended or repealed and that fact has not yet been noted in a pocket part or free-standing supplement. The last step in finding the current print statutory materials should be to look at the end of the entire *Tennessee Code Annotated* set for softbound "Advance Legislative Service" books, which will include tables showing how the most recently-passed legislation affects the current code.

---

7. Using electronic citator services to *update* your research is discussed more fully in Chapter 7.

3. Finding Cases that Interpret or Apply Statutes

It is rare to locate a relevant statute and be able to apply it immediately to your client's facts without having first researched case law. Legislatures write statutes with broad terms meant to apply to a wide array of circumstances. To be able to predict how a particular court will apply a statute to your client's particular facts, you must know how that court has interpreted the statute and applied it in the past.

After each statute in the *Tennessee Code Annotated*, under the heading "Notes to Decisions," are summaries of cases that have applied or interpreted the statute. The case summaries in the "Notes to Decisions" sections are organized by topic, and within each topic, the summaries are arranged by court and then by date. The summaries are each followed by a citation to the reporter or database where you can find the full text of the case. You must record this citation information accurately so that you can find the full text of any opinion that appears relevant to your facts.[8]

4. Other Helpful Features of the Tennessee Code Annotated

a. Additional Annotations

The *Tennessee Code Annotated* contains, after each statute, annotations and references to sources in addition to case opinions. Tennessee Attorney General opinions that interpret the statute and comments from administrative or legislative bodies involved in drafting the statute may be referenced. There are also cross-references to related statutes and references to secondary sources, such as practitioner's manuals and law review articles, that discuss the statute. These references provide a helpful starting point for further research.

---

8. If you are researching on LexisNexis or Westlaw, you will also find summaries of pertinent case decisions following statutes in the online version of the *Tennessee Code Annotated*. Instead of recording the citations to look up the cases later, you can usually follow a hyperlink to the full text of the opinion.

b. Statutory History

After the text of each statute, you will find the *statutory history line* (also called *statutory credits*), which tells when the statute was enacted, amended, and repealed. That line also provides citations to the session laws with the text of those acts that enacted, amended, or repealed the statute. Generally, the substantive law that will apply to a situation is the law that was in effect when the events happened. Thus, you must always check the statutory history line to be sure that the statute was in effect and has not been amended since the events you are researching took place. As an example, if you are researching the law on homicide with respect to a homicide that took place five years ago, you need to be sure that the law on homicide has not been amended in the intervening five years. If the homicide law had been amended in the intervening five years, you would have to re-search in archived code materials and the session laws to find the applicable version of the statutes.

Table 4-3 shows the statutory history line for Tenn. Code Ann. § 39-14-404, Especially Aggravated Burglary.

This statutory history line tells the researcher that the law was first passed in 1989, and the text of the original law can be found in the *Public and Private Acts of the State of Tennessee* for the year 1989, in Chapter 591, Section 1. The law was then amended in 1990, and the text of the amendment can be found in the *Public and Private Acts of the State of Tennessee* for 1990, in Chapter 1030, Section 24. Almost always, in statutory history lines, the punctuation that separates one reference to a session law from the next is a semi-colon. The first session law that appears in a statutory history line is a reference to the initial enactment of a law. The following references will be in chronological order, and will refer to amendments, re-numberings, or repeal of the law.

Table 4-3. Example Statutory History Line

[Acts 1989, ch. 591, § 1; 1990, ch. 1030, § 24.]

c. Tables

Volume 13 of the code set is the Tables volume, which allows researchers to translate former statute numbers to current statute numbers, and vice-versa. Several times in Tennessee history, the entire set of state statutes has been completely re-numbered. Thus, a case opinion from the 1950's will contain citations to statutes that bear little or no relation to the current statutory numbering scheme. To find the current statute that relates to the statute cited in the 1950's, use the Tables volume to look up the old citation and find a reference to the current statute.

The Tables volume also includes mortality, annuity, and valuation tables that are referenced in the Code. In addition, a chart of Tennessee counties and municipalities shows where to find their charters in the *Tennessee Code Annotated* or the *Public and Private Acts of the State of Tennessee.*

d. Rules

The last two volumes of the *Tennessee Code Annotated* contain procedural rules and rules of evidence. Both are important for lawyers practicing in Tennessee courts, as explained below in Part III.

C. Researching the Statutes of Other States

While the same basic process applies to statutory research in other states, some important differences deserve note. Some states' statutes are like Tennessee's in their numbering system: a three-part number, with the first number designating the title, the second number designating the chapter, and the third number designating the section. Other states simply give each statute one number, such as the *Kentucky Revised Statutes*, which may be cited as, for example, Ky. Rev. Stat. Ann. §525.125. Texas and some other states include both a subject title and a section number. The statute regarding alienation of affections lawsuits in Texas is located in Section

1.107 of the Texas Family Code. The citation is Tex. Fam. Code Ann. § 1.107.

Other states may have slightly different forms of publication. Some states republish their entire statutory code every year or every other year, rather than supplementing annually with pocket parts. Some states' statutory code sets include the annotations in a separate volume or volumes at the end of the set, rather than after each individual statute. Finally, some states' statutory codes include items such as official jury instructions or forms to be used in filing with their court system.

D. Federal Statutes

The official text of federal statutes is published in the *United States Code* (U.S.C.). Federal statutes are codified in the U.S.C. in fifty titles. Within each title, individual statutes are assigned section numbers. To cite a federal statute, you must include both the title and the section number. The federal statute granting appellate jurisdiction to federal appellate courts is 28 U.S.C. § 1291. Title 28 of the code is devoted to courts and judicial matters, and 1291 is the section number assigned to this statute.

The official *United States Code* is updated infrequently and does not include annotations, so it is of limited value in research. The sources you are more likely to use are the *United States Code Annotated* (U.S.C.A.), published by West, and the *United States Code Service* (U.S.C.S.), published by LexisNexis. While you will ordinarily cite to the U.S.C., since it is the official version of the code, you should cite to U.S.C.A. or U.S.C.S. if the current text of the statute is not available in the U.S.C.

Both U.S.C.S. and U.S.C.A. contain the text of federal statutes and references to related research sources. Both U.S.C.S. and U.S.C.A. include annotations that refer the researcher to cases interpreting or applying each federal statute. Some researchers find that U.S.C.A. provides more case annotations than U.S.C.S., while U.S.C.S. provides more helpful tables and better information on court rules. For the beginning researcher, both are probably of equal value. In practice, only one is likely to be available in a private library, so use whichever one you have access to.

U.S.C.A. and U.S.C.S. are updated through pocket parts and paperback supplements, just as is the *Tennessee Code Annotated.* To be certain that you have the current statutory language and the most recent annotations, check the pocket part or free-standing supplemental volume, as well as additional paperback supplements, called Advance Services, found at the end of each set. When only portions of the statute have changed, the pocket part may contain only the new, amended sections of the statute, and refer the reader back to the hardbound volume for the unchanged language in the original statute. Some pocket parts, though, will reprint the modified statute in full.

Both U.S.C.A. and U.S.C.S. contain information other than statutes and references to case opinions and secondary authorities. They provide references to federal regulations, executive orders, and legislative history materials. They also include helpful tables, such as tables listing statutes by their popular names (e.g., the USA PATRIOT Act and Megan's Law). And, as explained in the next part, both contain federal court rules.

U.S.C.A. can also be found on Westlaw, while U.S.C.S. can be found on LexisNexis. These online versions provide for easier access, via hyperlinking, to many of the materials summarized and referenced in the annotations to the code. Both LexisNexis and Westlaw also provide online versions of many of their tables and charts, such as popular names tables. Westlaw also features an online version of the statutory index to browse or search.

Unannotated versions of the federal statutes can also be found online for free. These versions vary in their levels of currency, accuracy, and ease of use. Test different versions of the code to see which you find easiest to navigate and always scrutinize the web version to see when it was last updated. Some sites which publish the United States Code for free include the House of Representatives Office of Law Revision Counsel, http://uscode.house.gov, the Government Printing Office, www.gpoaccess.gov/uscode/, Cornell

Law School's Legal Information Institute, www.law.cornell.edu/ uscode/, and Findlaw.com, www.findlaw.com/casecode/uscodes/.

III. Court and Ethical Rules

Court and ethical rules are frequently published in, or as companions to, statutory codifications. Court rules govern litigation practice from the filing of initial pleadings through the conclusion of the final appeal. Rules dictate procedural requirements ranging from the correct caption for pleadings to the standard for summary judgment. Court rules like the Tennessee Rules of Civil Procedure and the Tennessee Supreme Court Rules are primary authority even when the court or legislature responsible for them has delegated rule-making power to a council, committee, or other body. Success in litigation may depend as much on compliance with these rules as on the merits of the claim.

A. Tennessee Court Rules

As noted above, the *Tennessee Code Annotated* includes separate volumes that contain the Tennessee Rules of Civil Procedure, the Tennessee Rules of Criminal Procedure, and other procedural rules for various court systems in Tennessee. These rules are available in other sources as well. A compilation of rules is often referred to as a *deskbook*. West publishes a set of deskbooks for each state. The West deskbook for Tennessee is the *Tennessee Court Rules*. This particular set has three volumes. The first contains Tennessee federal court rules, for example, *Local Rules of the United States District Court for the Eastern District of Tennessee*. The second volume contains Tennessee state court rules, such as the *Tennessee Rules of Evidence*. The third volume contains local rules, such as the *Sixth Judicial District Local Rules of Practice (Knox County)*. For some states, the West deskbook set has only two volumes, for federal and state court rules, and omits the third volume of local rules.

Some rules are available online. The website of the Tennessee Administrative Office of the Courts, www.tncourts.gov, provides a

"Court Rules" link with links to most of the statewide court rules sets, some local (county-wide) rules, as well as proposed new rules and amendments. The rules available on this free website are accessible through hyperlinked tables of contents rather than being searchable or indexed. Tennessee rules are also available on LexisNexis and Westlaw. See the Appendix to Chapter 9 for more details.

Rules are written in outline form like statutes, and they should be read like statutes. Read each word carefully, refer to cross-referenced rules, and scan other rules nearby to see if they are related.

After finding a rule on point, look for cases that apply it. Usually the first step in looking for cases that apply a rule is to locate an annotated version of the rule, which will include summaries of, and citations to, case opinions. The rules published as part of the *Tennessee Code Annotated* are, as the name indicates, annotated with references to related cases. The West deskbook set, *Tennessee Court Rules*, is not annotated. You may also be able to find related case opinions by looking in the *Tennessee Digest* or in practitioner's manuals or other secondary sources. Never assume that a Tennessee rule precisely mirrors its federal counterpart, or that cases applying a federal rule will be relevant to the application of a Tennessee rule.

The text of some rules is accompanied by commentary from the committee charged with drafting or amending the rules. The commentary is persuasive authority.

Be sure that you are working with the current rule. West's deskbooks are published yearly, so they are reasonably current. The court rules volumes published with the *Tennessee Code Annotated* are also published yearly. Usually the first source to publish the most recent court rules and amendments is the website of the Tennessee Administrative Office of the Courts. The newsletter *Tennessee Attorneys Memo* may also include the text of important new court rules and amendments.

B. Federal Court Rules

Similar rules exist on the federal level. They are published in *Tennessee Rules of Court: Federal* as well as in U.S.C., U.S.C.A., and

U.S.C.S. Placement of the rules within each statutory publication varies. Sometimes the rules are integrated with the volumes of statutes for Title 28; other times the rules are in separate volumes at the end of the entire code. Each federal circuit and district court may have its own local rules with specific practices required by that court. Local rules for Tennessee's federal courts are found in the *Tennessee Rules of Court: Federal* volume. This volume contains local rules for the Sixth Circuit and for all the federal district courts and bankruptcy courts in Tennessee. A looseleaf series, *Federal Local Court Rules*, compiles all federal local court rules from across the country and is a helpful source if you have access to it. Some federal local court rules are available on the Internet as well as on LexisNexis or Westlaw.

Cases relevant to federal court rules can be found using the annotated codes, or by referring to the *Federal Practice Digest*, the *Federal Rules Service*, and the *Federal Rules of Evidence Service*. There are also in-depth treatises on federal procedure and rules that provide extensive citations to cases interpreting and applying federal rules.[9]

C. Professional Rules

The conduct of lawyers in Tennessee is regulated by the Rules of Professional Conduct, which are found in Rule 8 of the *Tennessee Supreme Court Rules.* The chapters of the Rules of Professional Conduct are set out in Table 4-4. These rules can be found in volume 2 of the paperbound "rules" volumes at the end of the *Tennessee Code Annotated*, in the West deskbook *Tennessee Rules of Court: State*, and on the internet at the Tennessee Administrative Office of the Courts site, www.tncourts.gov (click on "Court Rules," then "Current Rules," then "Supreme Court Rules").

The version of the Rules of Professional Conduct printed with the *Tennnessee Code Annotated* is, in fact, annotated, and includes refer-

---

9. For example, James Wm. Moore et al., *Moore's Federal Practice* (3d ed. 1997) and Charles A. Wright & Arthur R. Miller, *Federal Practice and Procedure* (2005).

Table 4-4. Chapters of the Rules of Professional Conduct

1. The Client-Lawyer Relationship
2. The Lawyer as Counselor, Intermediary, and Dispute Resolution Neutral
3. Advocate
4. Transactions with Persons Other Than Clients
5. Law Firms, Legal Departments, and Legal Service Organizations
6. Public Service
7. Information About Legal Services
8. Maintaining the Integrity of the Profession

ences to related Formal Ethics Opinions of the Tennessee Board of Professional Responsibility, judicial opinions, and law review articles. Because Tennessee adopted a new ethical code in 2003, many of the references are to opinions and articles written with respect to the prior ethical code. While the former and current codes share some similarities and language, authorities written interpreting and enforcing the old code will be considered persuasive as to the new code rather than mandatory.

Like most other jurisdictions, Tennessee adopted these new rules using the American Bar Association's *Model Rules of Professional Conduct* as a blueprint. The new rules were originally proposed by the Tennessee Bar Association, and the drafts of the proposed new rules were the subject of much study and debate. Many of the reports and comments regarding the new rules are available on the Tennessee Bar Association's website at www.tba.org/committees/conduct/.

Because these new rules were based on the *Model Rules of Professional Conduct*, opinions from other jurisdictions interpreting those rules adopted by Tennessee may be considered helpful persuasive authority, particularly if a Tennessee court or the Tennessee Board of Professional Responsibility has not spoken on the issue. You may wish to consult an annotated version of the ABA's *Model Rules of Professional Conduct* in order to find references to decisions from other jurisdictions.

Chapter 5

Legislative History

Researching Tennessee legislative history ... is a tedious and often-times fruitless task.[1]

This chapter covers the process by which the Tennessee General Assembly enacts statutes. It begins with an overview of the legislative process in Tennessee; through that process the statutory laws of Tennessee are enacted and changed.

Next, the chapter explains how to track changes to a bill during the legislative process and how to perform additional research on the *legislative intent* behind a statute that has already been enacted. As used here, *legislative intent research* involves any materials that might document why the legislature decided to pass a given law, or what the legislature intended the statute to mean or to do. Legislative intent research is most often relevant in litigation, when trying to convince a court to interpret an ambiguous statute in a way that is favorable to a client's position.

Next, the chapter describes how to track bills that are currently pending in the General Assembly.[2] Lawyers frequently track current bills that may affect a client's interests, or that may have an impact on an industry or profession which the lawyer frequently represents.

Finally, the chapter presents some brief information on researching federal legislative history and intent. The Appendices to this chapter present additional summarized information on how to access both Tennessee and federal legislative materials.

---

1. Office of Legal Services for the Tennessee General Assembly, *Legislative Drafting Manual* 95 (2003). Tennessee, when compared to many other states and to the federal government, creates and retains very little legislative history material. What material there is can be tricky to access.
2. How to use a statutory history line to track passed amendments to a statute is discussed in Chapter 4.

I. The Legislative Process

The Tennessee General Assembly consists of a Senate, with thirty-three members, and a House of Representatives, with ninety-nine members. The General Assembly meets for regular sessions every year, typically from January through May, though fiscal or other legislative crises may occasionally keep the legislature in session through July. The typical process of enacting laws in Tennessee is similar to that of other states and of the United States Congress. Table 5-1 shows the basic progression of an idea from bill to statute and notes the documents that are important in legal research.

Table 5-1. How a Bill Becomes a Law

Legislative Action	Documents Produced
An idea for legislation is suggested by a citizen, group, or legislator. A legislator sponsors the bill, and either drafts the language of the bill or has the General Assembly's Office of Legal Services draft the bill.	The text of a bill is important; if enacted, the bill's requirements or prohibitions may affect a client's interests. Even if a modified version is passed, comparing the original to the final version can help determine the legislature's intent.
The bill is introduced in either the House or Senate. The Tennessee Constitution requires that bills be considered and passed three times before becoming law. Typically, a bill is introduced and considered for the first time on the same day. If passed, it will be held for second consideration on the next legislative day. After being considered and passed a second time, the Speaker will refer the bill to a legislative committee for hearings or other action.	The bills that are introduced can be found in the *Tennessee House Bills* and the *Tennessee Senate Bills*.

After a bill has been referred to committee, it will remain there (a result commonly known as "dying in committee") unless one of several courses of action is followed to bring it out.[3] The committee may hold public hearings on the bill.

Since the late 1980's, the Tennessee State Library & Archives has been recording hearings held by the standing committees of the General Assembly.

The bill may be passed by the committee, passed with recommended amendments, or rejected or may otherwise die in committee. If the bill is passed, it goes back to the scheduling committee of either the House (the House Committee on Calendar and Rules) or the Senate (the Senate Calendar Committee). The House committee has the power to determine whether a bill will ever be scheduled for third consideration, while the Senate committee is prescribed to schedule every bill referred to it for a vote on the floor of the full Senate.

Audio tapes of floor proceedings are available from the Tennessee State Library & Archives. Votes are available in the journals of the House and Senate. Passed amendments to bills can be found in the *Tennessee House Bills* and *Tennessee Senate Bills*.

Typically, identical bills are introduced simultaneously in both houses. These bills are called companion bills. If the two companion bills have been amended so that they differ from each other, a conference committee may be appointed to attempt to reconcile the bills. Eventually, both houses must pass identical versions of the bill in order for it to be sent to the Governor.

The bill that is passed by both houses is the enrolled bill.

---

3. For a detailed explanation of those courses of action, see Tennessee General Assembly Legislative Information Services, *How a Bill Becomes a Law,* www.legislature.state.tn.us/info/billtolaw.htm.

If the Governor signs the bill, it becomes law. If the Governor does not sign the bill within ten days, it becomes law without signature. If the Governor vetoes the bill, the legislature may override with a simple majority vote in both houses.	
An enacted bill is assigned a session law number; in Tennessee this is called a chapter number. This is a chronological number based on when the bill was passed in that session of the legislature.	Session laws are published, at the end of each legislative session, in numerical order in *Tennessee Public Laws* and *Tennessee Private Laws*. They are also available almost immediately on the Tennessee legislature's website, www.legislature.state.tn.us.
The law is codified, meaning that it is assigned a number that places it with other laws on similar topics.	Tennessee statutes are officially codified in the *Tennessee Code Annotated* and unofficially codified in *West's Tennessee Code Annotated*.

II. Legislative History

Legislative history research is needed when the meaning of a statute is not clear from the text or context of the statute. It is especially useful for new legislation that has not yet been interpreted by the courts. When a statute does not explicitly address a given situation, reviewing the legislative history may assist in the effort to determine the legislature's intent in enacting the statute. For example, in *Worley v. Weigel's, Inc.*, 919 S.W.2d 589 (Tenn. 1996), the Tennessee Supreme Court reviewed statements made by the sponsor of a law during its enactment process in the legislature in order to determine how the statute should be applied to the litigants in the case.[4]

---

4. *Worley*, 919 S.W.2d at 593–94. Not all courts or judges are receptive to legislative intent or history arguments. Justice Antonin Scalia is probably the most well-known advocate of the "textualists." They believe that looking beyond the text of the given statute and its relation to the larger code, to the supposed "intent" of a multi-membered legislative body, is an inherently flawed method of determining how a statute should be read.

A. Tracking Historical Bills

During the legislative process, the General Assembly may consider many different proposed versions of a bill, as well as amendments to the bill. The language in the bill and its amendments that the General Assembly accepts, when compared to the language which it rejects, can help provide lawyers and courts with clues as to what the legislature intended the statute to do. For example, in *Chapman v. Sullivan County*, 608 S.W.2d 580 (Tenn. 1980), the Tennessee Supreme Court examined amendments to a bill during the legislative process to clarify the definition of a "governmental entity" under the Tennessee Governmental Tort Liability Act.

Reconstructing a bill's journey through both houses of the General Assembly can be time-consuming and requires particular attention to detail, but once you are familiar with the sources used and the steps involved, the process is not terribly difficult. Table 5-2 outlines the procedure for tracing a previously-enacted statute through its legislative beginnings.

Table 5-2. Tracking a Passed Bill

Step	Result
1. Check the statutory history line to determine the Public Chapter citation for the law as it was first passed. Each statute's statutory history line is found at the end of the statute in brackets.	The statutory history line for Tenn. Code Ann. §36-5-2611, [Acts 1997, ch. 551, §2], indicates that the law was first passed in 1997, and the text of the original law can be found in the 1997 *Public Acts of the State of Tennessee*, chapter 551, section 2.
2. Locate the original law in the *Public Acts* and note the House and Senate bill numbers associated with the Act. The House and Senate bill numbers are listed at the very beginning of the Act, in the caption at the top.	Examining chapter 551 of the Tennessee *Public Acts* reveals that it was introduced as House Bill No. 1818 and Senate Bill No. 1707.

3. Look up the text of the original bill, and all amendments to it that were passed, in the *Tennessee House Bills* and *Tennessee Senate Bills*. These sets are organized by year/legislative session and then, within those volumes, by bill number. In the *House Bills*, the original bill is printed on yellow paper, and amendments on blue. In the *Senate Bills*, the original bill is printed on green paper, with amendments on blue.

Studying the *Tennessee House Bills* and *Tennessee Senate Bills* shows that the original proposed law was a very simple change to the child support and enforcement laws. In a Senate Committee, it was substantially amended and the proposed law eventually rewrote the entire portion of the *Tennessee Code Annotated* dealing with child support and enforcement.

4. Move to the *Senate Journal* and *House Journal* for the legislative session involved. Most legislative sessions result in two volumes of journals for each house. At the end of the final volume for each legislative session, there is a table, arranged by bill number, indicating where in each *Journal* a researcher will find any action on the bill.

The closing tables for the *Senate Journal* and the *House Journal* (see Table 5-3) specify each page in each journal where the original bills were referenced or voted upon. Checking these references reveals that House Bill 1810 was also involved in the creation of Acts 1997, ch. 551.

5. Return to the *Tennessee House Bills* and look up the text of House Bill 1810.

House Bill 1810 also was substantially amended during its course through the General Assembly.

6. Move back to the *House Journal* and check the closing tables for information on House Bill 1810.

On the third and final consideration of House Bill 1810, several amendments, and amendments to amendments, were proposed and adopted. One amendment was withdrawn. The final version of H.B. 1810 passed unanimously.

Researching a bill that was introduced but never passed, as long as you know the bill number, works almost precisely the same way as outlined in Table 5-2. The exception is that you can skip the first two steps and proceed directly to the bill collections and the House and Senate journals. Table 5-3 is a page from a *House Journal* showing the entry for House Bill 1810, mentioned in step six above. If you do not know the bill number, subject indexes are available starting from 1963. The *Unofficial Index to Legislation Introduced in the General Assembly* was published in print from 1963 through 1995. This index was discontinued when the legislature began publishing bills on the Internet. So, for more recent bills, researchers must go to the Tennessee General Assembly's web page at www.legislature.state.tn.us. Click "Legislation," then "Archive," then select which legislative session to search, and then search by key word.

B. Additional Resources for Tennessee Legislative History Research

You may need to find legislative history materials beyond amendments to and votes on a bill in the General Assembly. Another way to discover the possible intent of the General Assembly in passing or amending a bill is to listen to tapes of debates on the floors of the respective houses and of committee meetings. These tapes are available from the Tennessee State Library & Archives. In order to locate tapes of pertinent debates and committee meetings, have the Public Act number and/or the bill numbers and the year involved, and contact the Legislative History staff at (615) 741–1549. The staff will conduct research to find available tapes and indexes to the tapes (also called *log sheets*). Once a list of available materials is generated, the researcher may then choose to listen to the tapes at the State Library & Archives in Nashville, or to have copies made and delivered to an outside location. There is a fee for this research service and for having tape duplicates made.

Occasionally, committee members of the state legislature will have printed materials, such as reports on bills or research reviews, delivered to the State Library & Archives as well. These printed materials

Table 5-3. Excerpt from *House Journal*

Number	SPONSOR	DESCRIPTION	Passed First Consideration	Passed Second Consideration	SB Page / Senate Bill Substituted	Passed Third Consideration	Passed by Senate	Signed by Speaker of House	Signed by Speaker of Senate	Signed by Governor	OTHER ACTION	CHAPTER NUMBER
1806	McDaniel, et al	Authorizes index of appropriations from state tax revenues for 1996-1997 fiscal year to exceed $55 million or 0.84 percent.	442	492		1842	2205	2402	2403	2404	408, 756, 777, 1355, 1551, 1694, 1897, 2017, 2034, 2036, 2196, 2258, 2292, 2294, 2402, 2403	512
1807	McDaniel, et al	Authorizes index of appropriations from state tax revenues for 1997-1998 fiscal year to exceed $10 million or 0.15 percent.	443	492	945						408	
1808	McKee, et al	Defines "covered security" and "senior security", sets out new conditions for security sales and investment advising; mandates notice filings for covered security sales.	443	492	1700						408, 603, 754, 868	
1809	Haleman Harwel, et al	Reschedules deadline from October 1 to October 15 for commissioner to report to governor and general assembly regarding projected standard of need annual adjustments for temporary assistance program.	443	492							408	
1810	Stamps, et al	Revises child support and paternity law to conform with new federal guidelines; enacts "Uniform Interstate Family Support Act."	443	492		2037	2309	2402	2403	2405	408	551
1811	Kent, et al	Enacts "Office of Film, Music & Multimedia Industries Act of 1997."	443	492							408, 562, 669	
1812	Wood, et al	Enacts "Interstate Contracting for Federal Programs Act."	443	492	1937 1280						408, 1109, 1234	
1813	Wood, et al	Renames department of labor as department of labor and workforce development.	443	493							408	
1814	Kisber, et al	Gives sales and use tax credit for building materials, machinery and equipment used in construction of qualified, new or expanded corporate headquarters located in state; currently, FedEx facility in Collierville meets qualifications.	443	493		872	1099	1103	1126	1258	408, 747, 754, 811, 847, 860, 866, 883, 1103, 1126	178
1815	Haley, et al	Prohibits issuance of new registration plates by commissioner of safety prior to 1/17/2000; thereafter, plates to be issued on each fifth anniversary.	443	493		1050	1128	2402	2403	2404	409, 562, 671, 937, 1017, 1044, 1067, 1128, 2402, 2403	538

Column group heading over the action columns: **HOUSE BILLS** (of which there are very few) are generally accessible only at the State Library & Archives in Nashville. Some recent materials may also be available on Westlaw in the TN-LH (Tennessee Legislative History) database.

The paucity of accessible materials on Tennessee legislative history is a stark contrast to what legal researchers have available for most other states and certainly for federal legislative materials. Federal legislative history materials are discussed briefly in Part IV of this chapter. A guide to web pages discussing legislative history and intent research for all fifty states is compiled and maintained at the Indiana University School of Law Library.[5] Another valuable resource for learning about legislative history and tracking research in all fifty states is the *State Legislative Sourcebook*.[6]

III. Tracking Current Bills

Of the many bills that are introduced in each legislative session, some may affect the rights of a client by proposing new laws or amending existing laws. In advising a client, an attorney needs to learn of any bills on topics relevant to the client's interest and follow their progress through the process outlined above.

A. Researching with a Bill Number

If you know the number of a current bill that you need to track, you can do so easily on the Tennessee legislature's website at no charge. The address is www.legislature.state.tn.us. From that opening page, click on the "Legislation" link in the left hand frame, then "Filed Bills Index" from the ensuing drop-down menu. For information on

---

5. *See* Jennifer Bryan Morgan, *State Legislative History Guides on the Web*, www.law.indiana.edu/library/services/sta_leg.shtml.

6. Lynn Hellebust, *State Legislative Sourcebook: A Resource Guide to Legislative Information in the Fifty States 2006* (2006).

bills from previous legislative sessions, instead of clicking on the "Filed Bills Index" link, choose "Archive." The materials available go back to 1995.

After you click on "Filed Bills Index," you may have an option to choose between two or more of the most recent legislative sessions. Choose which session you want to research. From there, you will be presented with links to all bills and resolutions filed, arranged in numerical order. Clicking on the link for the bill you are researching will take you first to a tracking page. That page includes the following:

- A concise summary of the bill's topic and language;
- A reference to the portion of the *Tennessee Code Annotated* that would be amended or repealed by enactment of the bill;
- Links to the full text of the bill, and any amendments, in .pdf format;
- Links to any fiscal notes explaining the financial impact of enactment of the bill;
- If the bill has been enacted, a link to the official version of the *public chapter* (session law); and
- A history showing all legislative action taken on the bill (referrals to committees, amendments, and the like).

B. Learning About Other Pending Bills

If you know of a bill that you want to track but do not know the bill number, or if you need to learn whether there even might be pending legislation that affects your work, you have a few different options. If you are working entirely with free Internet resources, you can go to the Tennessee Legislature's home page at www.legislature .state.tn.us and click on "Legislation" in the left hand frame. Now, in the main portion of the screen, you will have an option to "Search All Documents for Keyword." You can use this search box to look for documents containing a particular word or phrase (for example, "*covenant marriage*") or for a *Tennessee Code Annotated* section number. Searching for a section number should allow you to find any pending bills that would affect that particular section. For example, if you are interested in learning whether pending legislation might affect Tenn. Code Ann. §63-1-117, you could enter "63-1-117" as your search phrase to retrieve a list of pending bills that reference section 63-1-117. Be sure to use quotation marks, as otherwise the search software will retrieve anything that has the number 63, the number 1, or the number 117.

If you have access to Westlaw, the KeyCite system (explained in more depth in Chapter 7) will let you find pending legislation that affects your statute. Once you have retrieved your statute on Westlaw, look for the KeyCite graphical symbol towards the top of the statute. A yellow flag may mean that current legislation is pending that would amend or repeal the statute. A red flag could mean that legislation that amends or repeals your statute has been very recently passed. If you see a yellow or red flag, you can click on it to find links to the legislation. You can also use KeyCite Alert to receive emails from Westlaw about any legislation introduced later that would affect your statute. Appendix 1 to this chapter explains how to access some of the legislative databases found on Westlaw and LexisNexis in more detail.

IV. Federal Legislative Research

A. Federal Legislative History

Researching federal legislative history involves roughly the same steps as researching Tennessee's laws, though some of the terminology is different and more types of materials are available. Bills are numbered sequentially in each chamber of Congress. Generally, Senate bills are preceded by an "S," and House bill numbers are preceded by "H.R." When a federal statute is enacted, it is printed as a small booklet and assigned a *public law number*. This number is in the form Pub. L. No. 108-187. The first part of this public law number, 108, refers to the 108th Congress. The second part of this public law number, 187 indicates that this slip law was the 187th law passed by the 108th Congress. The public law number given above is for the *Can Spam Act*, which set national standards for sending commercial e-mail.

The new statute is later published as a *session law* in *United States Statutes at Large*, which is the federal counterpart of the *Public Acts of the State of Tennessee*. Session laws are designated by volume and page in *Statutes at Large*, e.g., 117 Stat. 2699. Finally, the new law is assigned a *statute number* (or numbers) when it is codified with statutes on similar topics in the *United States Code*. The citation for the first section of the Can Spam Act is 15 U.S.C. §7701.

As with Tennessee legislative history, federal legislative history research begins with a statute number. If you do not know the statute number, use an annotated code to find it (as described in Chapter 4). With a statute number, you can find the citation to the *Statutes at Large* (session laws) and to the public law number, which lead to the legislative history of the bill as it worked its way through Congress.

1. Sources of Federal Legislative History

In conducting federal legislative history research, you are primarily looking for committee reports, materials from committee hearings, and transcripts of floor debates.[7] Committee reports are usually considered the most persuasive authority, since they represent the judgment and opinion of the committee, usually rendered after extensive hearings, with witness testimony and lengthy submissions of exhibits and statements about the bill. Congressional committee reports are often lengthy documents, published as soft-cover books. They can also be found published in a hardbound set commonly called the *Serial Set* or the *United States Serial Set*, archived in various microfiche collections, and in searchable format in different online databases. These reports contain the committee's analysis of the bill, the reasons for enacting it, and the views of committee members who disagree with those reasons.[8]

---

7. More detailed information on how to access these materials can be found in Appendix 2 at the end of this chapter.

Congressional hearing materials include transcripts from the proceedings as well as documents such as prepared testimony and exhibits.

Floor debates are published in the *Congressional Record*. Be wary in relying on these debates, as they may not have actually been delivered in the House or Senate; members of Congress can amend their remarks and even submit written statements that are published in transcript form as if they were spoken.[9]

Table 5-4 compares sources for Tennessee and federal legislative history.

2. *Compiled Legislative History*

Some researchers have compiled legislative history for certain federal statutes. Two reference books that index compiled legislative histories of major federal statutes are *Sources of Compiled Legislative Histories*[10] and *Federal Legislative Histories*.[11] Individual legislative histories may also be found by searching the online catalog at a law library. Perform key word searches using the name of the act and the public law number as search terms.

---

8. *United States Code Congressional and Administrative News* (often referred to as "USCCAN") is a print source of selected legislative history materials which contains the text of the enacted bills and excerpts of the more instructive committee reports. Materials in USCCAN can be accessed by public law number. *United States Code Annotated* will often include citations to relevant pages in USCCAN.

9. In a notorious political scandal, in November 2005, lobbyist Michael Scanlon pleaded guilty to bribing members of Congress. One of the things he paid Rep. Bob Ney (R-Oh.) to do was to insert remarks in the *Congressional Record* favorable to the purchase of a line of gambling boats by Scanlon's business partner, lobbyist Jack Abramoff. James V. Grimaldi & Susan Schmidt, "Lawmaker's Abramoff Ties Investigated," Wash. Post, Oct. 18, 2005, at A01; and Philip Shenon, "Former Top Aide to DeLay Pleads Guilty to Conspiracy," N.Y. Times, Nov. 22, 2005, at A21.

10. Nancy P. Johnson, *Sources of Compiled Legislative Histories: A Bibliography of Government Documents, Periodical Articles, and Books* (Am. Ass'n of Law Libraries, Publ. Series No. 14, 2000).

11. Bernard D. Reams, Jr., *Federal Legislative Histories: An Annotated Bibliography and Index to Officially Published Sources* (1994 & Supp. 2003).

Table 5-4. Comparison of Sources for Tennessee and Federal
Legislative History

Action	Tennessee Sources	Federal Sources
Committee work	Audio tapes of committee meetings	Reports written by committees are the most persuasive form of legislative history. Transcripts of hearing and evidentiary documents may also be available.
Debate	Audio tapes of floor debates; some mention of topics of discussion may occasionally be found in the *House Journal* and the *Senate Journal*.	*Congressional Record* publishes the statements of Senators and House members during debate.
Session laws	Recent *Tennessee Acts* are published online at the state legislature's web page. Hardbound volumes of *Tennessee Public Acts* and *Tennessee Private Acts* are published after each legislative session.	*Statutes at Large* is the official print publication of federal session laws. They are also available online from the Government Printing Office.
Codified version	*Tennessee Code Annotated* (official) *West's Tennessee Code Annotated* (unofficial)	*United States Code* (official) *United States Code Annotated* (unofficial) *United States Code Service* (unofficial)

B. Tracking Current Federal Bills and Recently Passed Laws on the Internet

More Congressional material is available daily via the Internet, and using Internet sources for bill tracking is often easier than using print sources. The Library of Congress site at http://thomas.loc.gov provides bill text, summaries, and status; committee reports; and the *Congressional Record* (which records debate in the House and Senate). The materials are organized in an easy-to-use format, so that once you find the bill or law that you are researching, it is simple to link to related reports and debates. The Government Printing Office site at www.gpoaccess.gov contains similar materials. Coverage varies even within a single site, so check the available dates and materials carefully.

Appendix 1
Tennessee Legislative History Materials

Item	Selected Sources & Availability
Tennessee bills and amendments	*Tennessee House Bills* and *Tennessee Senate Bills* in print. Current bills at www.legislature.state.tn.us/bills/currentga/billLookup.asp. Bills from 99th General Assembly forward at: www.legislature.state.tn.us (select Legislation, then Archive). TN-BILLS for current bills on Westlaw, and TN-BILLS-OLD for bills dating back to 1995 on Westlaw. On LexisNexis, select "Tennessee," then "Statutes & Regulations" for bills and the legislative archive.
Tennessee committee reports and legislative analyses	Typically not available. Check with the Tennessee State Library & Archives or search the TN-LH database on Westlaw.
Transcripts of Tennessee General Assembly committee hearings	Tape recordings available from the Tennessee State Library & Archives.

Appendix 1
Tennessee Legislative History Materials, cont'd

Item	Selected Sources & Availability
Records of floor votes and amendments for Tennessee bills	*Tennessee House Journal* and *Tennessee Senate Journal* in print.
Witness statements and evidentiary documents from Tennessee committee hearings	Typically not available. Check with the Tennessee State Library & Archives.
Transcripts of debates from the floor of the houses of the Tennessee General Assembly	Tape recordings available from the Tennessee State Library & Archives.
Tracking for current Tennessee bills	Online at www.legislature.state.tn.us/ (click "Legislation" in left column). On Westlaw, TN-BILLTRK. On LexisNexis, select Tennessee, then "TN Bill Tracking and Full-Text Bills."

Appendix 2
Federal Legislative History Materials

Item	Selected Sources & Availability
Federal bills and amendments	Older bills may be available on microfiche. To locate bills, use the *Final Cumulative Finding Aid, House and Senate Bills*, which is issued for each Congress.
	For recent bills, check the Library of Congress (http://loc.thomas.gov) (1989–present) or GPO (www.gpoaccess.gov/bills/index.html) (1993–present).
	LexisNexis: Select "Federal Legal," then "Legislative Histories & Materials," then "Congressional Full Text Bills," then "Current Congress." For archived materials, select "Federal Legal," then "Archived Bill Text & Tracking."
	Westlaw: CONG-BILLTXT database for current bills, CONG-BILLTXT-ALL database for material archived back to 1995.
	LexisNexis Congressional (also called Congressional Universe) subscription database (1989–present).
	Some bills are reprinted in the *Congressional Record* (see below) and in Congressional committee reports.
Congressional committee reports	In print in the *United States Congressional Serial Set* or as individual GPO publications. Selected excerpts from reports in *United States Code Congressional & Administrative News*.
	In microfiche from the Government Printing Office or from Congressional Information Service. ("C.I.S.")
	Online from GPO at www.gpoaccess.gov/serialset/creports/index.html (1995–present).
	LexisNexis: Select "Federal Legal," then "Legislative Histories & Materials," then "Committee Reports" (1990–present, selective coverage for earlier years).
	Westlaw: Legisliaive History database ("LH") for committee reports from 1990 and some selected excerpts from 1948–1990.
	LexisNexis Congressional has historical (1789–1969) committee reports available in .pdf format as part of the "Digital Serial Set."

Appendix 2
Federal Legislative History Materials, cont'd

Item	Selected Sources & Availability
Witness statements and evidentiary documents submitted at Congressional hearings	Typically included with Congressional committee reports.
Transcripts of Congressional committee hearings	May be published as individual documents and cataloged separately.
	On microfiche from C.I.S. Selected committee hearings online from GPO, 1995–forward, at www.gpoaccess.gov/chearings/index.html.
	Westlaw: USTESTIMONY database contains selected transcripts of witness testimony from Congressional hearings.
Congressional Record (transcript of Congressional debates and remarks, roll call votes, some full-text bills)	In print and microfiche from the GPO.
	Available online at www.gpoaccess.gov/crecord/index.html (GPO, 1994–present), http://thomas.loc.gov (Library of Congress, 1989–present), and Congressional Universe subscription database (1985–present).
	LexisNexis: Select "Federal Legal," then "Legislative Histories & Materials" (1985–current).
	Westlaw: CR database (1985–present).
Tracking for current federal bills	*Calendars of the United States House of Representatives* tracks daily movements of bills and resolutions. *Congressional Index* looseleaf set (published by Commerce Clearinghouse).
	Online at http://thomas.loc.gov/home/bills_res.html or www.govtrack.us.
	LexisNexis: Select "Federal Legal," then "Legislative Histories & Materials," then "Bill Tracking Report—Current Congress."
	Westlaw: US-BILLTRK database.

Chapter 6

Administrative Law

I. Administrative Law and Governmental Agencies

The regulations and decisions of administrative agencies are *administrative law*. Administrative law is primary authority. It is also mandatory, binding authority, assuming that it is on point and in the proper jurisdiction.

Administrative agencies include boards, commissions, and departments that are part of the executive branch of government.[1] Many of Tennessee's administrative agencies are established and described in Title 4, Chapter 3 of the *Tennessee Code Annotated*. Within the *Tennessee Code Annotated*, administrative agencies are usually referred to as "departments" or "divisions."

Agencies are administered by the executive branch, but agencies are usually established by the legislature through enabling statutes.[2] The statutory provisions that create agencies establish the powers and

---

1. An "agency" is "each state board, commission, committee, department, officer, or any other unit of state government authorized or required by any statute or constitutional provision to make rules or to determine contested cases." Tenn. Code Ann. §4-5-102(2) (2005). The term "contested cases" is further defined in the same statute to refer only to administrative cases. The judicial branch of government is not an "agency" because of this definition. Tenn. Code Ann. §4-5-103 (2005).

2. Some boards and commissions may be created by executive proclamation or order.

duties of the agencies. Each agency must work within the limits set by its enabling statute.

Each of the three branches of government has some oversight of agency functions. The legislative branch generally grants agencies the power to perform their duties and provides funding for the agencies to operate. The courts may determine whether the agencies' rules and opinions are valid. The executive branch supervises all state agencies and exercises control over some state agencies by appointing their highest officials.

In general, agencies function within the bounds of an Administrative Procedures Act (APA). Tennessee's APA is found at Tenn. Code Ann. §4-5-101 *et seq.* Note, however, that some agencies are exempt from all or parts of the Tennessee APA.[3] The APA requires the opportunity for the public to be notified of proposed rules and for the public to have the opportunity to comment upon them before they are adopted, except in some emergency circumstances. To meet this goal, agencies schedule public hearings where interested people may make suggestions or express concerns before a rule is finally adopted or changed. The APA also sets requirements for administrative hearings to make sure they are conducted fairly.[4]

Administrative law is unique because agencies perform functions of all three of the traditional branches of government. Agencies issue regulations[5] that interpret and define broader statutes. These regulations are similar in form, function, and authority to statutes enacted by the legislature. As part of the executive branch, agencies have the authority to enforce statutes and regulations, such as by issuing licenses (e.g., occupational licenses, driving licenses, and fishing li-

---

3. Tenn. Code. Ann. §4-5-106 (2005). For example, the state board of claims, the state election commission, and the board of probation and parole are all exempt from several provisions of Tennessee's APA.

4. Tenn Code. Ann. §§4-5-202 and 301 *et seq.*

5. Regulations are also frequently referred to as "rules." It is important to keep in mind the distinction between statutes on the one hand, and rules and regulations on the other hand. Referring to a statute as a "regulation" will be confusing or annoying to an educated legal audience.

censes), conducting investigations to see whether laws are being followed, and issuing orders to stop conduct that does not comport with the law.

Agencies also hold quasi-judicial hearings, deciding cases that involve the agency's rules or its mission. For example, state agencies hold hearings to determine whether an applicant is entitled to workers' compensation benefits or whether a doctor's license to practice should be suspended. These hearings are similar to court hearings. They are presided over by an administrative officer or administrative law judge. Each side may be represented by counsel, submit written briefs, and call witnesses to testify. However, the hearings are typically much less formal than court hearings.

Many lawyers devote much of their professional careers to practicing before administrative agencies and spend much of their legal research efforts finding, analyzing, and interpreting administrative materials. Many first-year law students do not see or hear much about administrative materials and are surprised at how intensively administrative materials are used and consulted in practice.

II. Administrative Regulations

Administrative agencies promulgate *regulations*, similar to the legislature enacting statutes. Administrative regulations are written in a format similar to statutes. Many regulations supply details that the legislature does not include in statutes, as demonstrated in Table 6-1. Since agencies are supposed to be the experts in particular legal areas, they can be well suited for supplying specific details to flesh out the more general statutes. Regulations may also provide guidance based on an agency's understanding of a relevant statute or determine procedural deadlines and format for agency filings.

Although regulations and statutes are both primary authority, regulations are subordinate to statutes. If there is any inconsistency between a regulation and a statute, the statute wins. A regulation cannot "cure" a statute that a court has held to be unconstitutional.

Table 6-1. Example of Relationship between Statutes and Regulations

Tennessee statutes governing eligibility for unemployment compensation often refer to "partial unemployment." A regulation issued by the Tennessee Department of Labor and Workforce Development, Tenn. Comp. R. & Regs. 0560-1-1-.11, defines "partial unemployment":

   (1) Partial employment presupposes that the worker is working less than full-time because the worker's employer is unable to provide the worker with full-time work.

   (2) A worker is partially unemployed only if the worker had a continuous attachment to an employer during a given claim period; in other words, during such period as the worker is "underemployed" and not "unemployed" in the sense that an individual has no employer.

   (3) To establish eligibility for partial benefits, an individual must be able and available for work during the period for which the individual is claiming the benefits.

Sources: *Tennessee Code Annotated* sections 50-7-302 and 50-7-303; *Official Compilation of the Rules and Regulations of the State of Tennessee* 0560-1-1-.11.

Administrative regulations in Tennessee are designated by a number in the form 0000-0-0.00. The first four digits are the agency chapter number. The regulation in Table 6-1 starts with 0560, which refers to the Department of Labor and Workplace Development. The second and third numbers work to group a related series of regulations together. In the above example, all of the Tennessee regulations that start with 0560-1-1 have to do with unemployment insurance benefits. Individual regulations in this chapter are then numbered from 0560-1-1-.01 through 0560-1-1-.26. Table 6-2 provides another example of the numbering of Tennessee regulations.

III. Researching Tennessee Administrative Law

The steps to take when researching administrative law will vary depending on the issue and how much information you have to start with. Table 6-3 outlines the steps broadly, but keep in mind that you may not need to take all of these steps in all situations.

Table 6-2. Example of Tennessee Administrative Regulation Numbering

The rules of the Tennessee Board of Regents are contained in Chapter 0240 of the *Official Compilation of the Rules and Regulations of the State of Tennessee*. Regulations are then grouped according to subject:

0240-1: Statewide Administrative Rules

0240-2: Systemwide Student Rules

0240-3: Institutional Student Disciplinary Rules

0240-4: Institutional Student Housing Rules

Within 0240-2, regulations at 0240-2-2 deal with classifying students as in-state or out-of-state. Regulation 0240-2-2-.04 describes out-of-state students who are not required to pay out-of-state tuition, and Regulation 0240-2-2-.07 deals with the procedure for students to appeal their classification as in-state or out-of-state.

Table 6-3. Researching Tennessee Administrative Regulations

1. Find the applicable regulation. Try searching the Tennessee regulations online, checking the web page of the agency involved, reviewing secondary sources, or calling an expert at the agency in question.

2. Research the enabling act. Check to see whether the agency acted within its power in promulgating the regulation. Check the text of the statute as well as cases and Attorney General opinions that interpret the statute.

3. Update your research to see if your regulation has been recently amended, rescinded, superseded, or otherwise changed.

4. Look for case opinions and agency decisions that interpret and apply the regulation.

5. If possible, speak with agency personnel about how the regulation has been interpreted and applied in the past, as well as any potential regulatory changes that may be pending.

A. Find the Applicable Regulation

1. *Availability of Tennessee Regulations*

Tennessee's regulations, the *Official Compilation of the Rules and Regulations of the State of Tennessee*, are published only electronically. The official version is published by Tennessee's Secretary of State and can be found at www.state.tn.us/sos/rules. This official version is published in .pdf format and is accessed by clicking through a series of menus. There is no way to search the entire *Official Compilation of the Rules and Regulations* using the version published by the Secretary of State.

Tennessee's regulations are more easily searchable in other electronic formats. These regulations are available on Westlaw in the TN-ADC database. On LexisNexis, access the Tennessee regulations database by clicking "Tennessee," then "TN – Rules and Regulations of the State of Tennessee."[6] They are also available on various CD-ROM products and in other subscription-based web research services.

2. *Searching for Tennessee Regulations*

A combination of browsing and searching may be necessary to find relevant regulations. Both LexisNexis and Westlaw provide tables of contents for the Tennessee regulations, so you can click through a table of links to find relevant regulations without having to enter specific search terms. If you are not sure which agency promulgated regulations that might impact your issue, or if you do not know which chapter of a given regulatory title might apply, try searching the database with key words instead. Possible key words for searching include the name of the agency involved (e.g., "Human Services"), any name

---

6. Check the database information carefully to see when it was last updated. You may also wish to check this "current-through" date against the free version available from the Secretary of State to see which one is more recent. The versions available from pay services such as Westlaw and LexisNexis are not necessarily more current than the free version available from the state government.

commonly used to refer to the regulations (e.g., "child support guidelines"), and words that might be included in the text of the regulation (such as "health insurance," "medical insurance," "medical expenses"). Which combinations of these searches will yield the best results varies depending on how the regulations are drafted and whether you are looking for regulations on a broad topic or those that address a specific factual situation.

Many administrative agencies in Tennessee provide direct links from their web pages to the regulations they have promulgated. When you are sure you know which agency is involved in your issue, it can save some time to find the regulations via the agency's web page. Using the agency's web page may also help streamline your research if the agency compiles links to related portions of the *Tennessee Code Annotated* together with the link to its regulations.

Another approach you may wish to consider is checking pertinent secondary sources to find references to Tennessee regulations. For example, Thomas A. Reynolds, *Tennessee Workers' Compensation Practice and Procedure*, in 20 *Tennessee Practice* (6th ed. 2005), includes discussion of workers' compensation regulations together with discussion of applicable statutes and case law. Using a secondary source as a starting point can be especially helpful if the source includes a Table of Laws and Regulations or similar finding aid. Typically, these tables are placed at the end of the work. Once you find a pertinent regulation, you can look up the regulation in the Table to see where else it is discussed in the book. This can lead to additional analysis and citations to related authorities.

Contacting an expert at the agency in question should also be considered when researching regulations. While this should not usually be a first step in regulatory research, consider it when you have taken the steps outlined above and feel that additional regulations or context may be needed. In most cases, agency staffers are pleased to speak with someone who is working and interested in their field. Do not expect that you can contact them and have them do your research, find the applicable regulations, and send them to you, but they may be able to tell you about possible new developments or point you in the general direction of related regulations that you had not yet found.

3. Reading Regulations and Their Notes

After finding references to on-point regulations, read the text of each regulation carefully. Many techniques used for reading statutes apply equally well to reading regulations. For example, when reading regulations you should always look for a separate regulation that provides definitions, be aware of cross-references, read the text several times, outline any complicated provisions, and check the table of contents for the chapter to make sure you have found other relevant regulations.

Following each individual regulation is an *authority note* and an *administrative history note*. The authority note refers the reader to the authority that empowered a state agency to issue that regulation. Usually this citation is to the *Tennessee Code Annotated* and the *Public and Private Acts of the State of Tennessee*. The administrative history note tells the history of that regulation, just as a statutory history line tells the history of its statute. This history can be important in determining when a regulation was promulgated, amended, repealed, or renumbered. Since the legal issue you are researching will be controlled by the regulations in effect when the issue arose, you need to read the administrative history note to learn of any changes to the regulation since that time. The administrative history lists in chronological order when the original regulation was filed and when it took effect, as well as all amendments, repeals, and issues of new regulations.

4. Finding Older Regulations

If your issue is governed by a past version of a regulation, locating that older regulation may prove difficult. Westlaw currently makes archived versions of the regulations available as far back only as 2002, and LexisNexis has archived versions available only from 2004 forward. The official version on the web is the current version only. Older regulations that have been repealed or amended are kept at the Tennessee State Library and Archives in Nashville and may be available in print, on microfilm, or on CD-ROM, depending on when they were published.

B. Research the Enabling Act

When researching administrative law, you may need to determine whether the agency acted within its power in issuing a given regulation, order, or decision. If that is in doubt, your first step in researching an administrative rule is to find the statute that gives the agency power to act. This statute is listed in the authority note following each regulation. The next step is to find cases that interpret the statute. This research will help determine whether the agency acted within the scope of its power in the situation that affects your client. Chapters 2, 3, and 4 of this book give guidance on researching case opinions, statutes, and constitutions. If the agency's power is not an issue, skip this inquiry and move directly to updating the regulations, as explained next.

C. Update Your Regulatory Research

When researching Tennessee regulations, you will need to determine whether new regulations or pending amendments could affect your client's issue. Chapter 7 deals with updating using citator services such as KeyCite and Shepard's. But KeyCite and Shepard's do not provide citation service for Tennessee regulations, so to update regulatory research, you will need to work a bit harder and be a bit more creative.

One way to check for very recent regulations or changes or additions to existing regulations is to stay current with the Secretary of State's regulations website, at www.state.tn.us/sos/rules/. This website includes links to recently-published regulations and emergency regulations. It also provides the option of subscribing to an RSS feed[7] of recently published and amended regulations, so that regulatory up-

---

7. RSS, which stands for Really Simple Syndication, allows subscribers to have updates on a particular topic sent to their computer. Subscribers must install an RSS Reader on their computer, then direct the reader to look for updates on the topics they have subscribed to by clicking an "update" button. RSS Readers are widely available on the Internet for free, and are not complicated to install or use.

dates can be searched for and downloaded with the click of a button. The website also has links to upcoming hearings on proposed regulatory changes.

Another way to access new regulations, proposed regulations, emergency regulations, and notices of rule-making hearings is to consult the *Tennessee Administrative Register* (commonly called TAR), which is published monthly. TAR is published only online. The official version is published by the Secretary of State and can be found at http://state.tn.us/sos/pub/tar/. As TAR does not have a compiled index to check, browse at least the table of contents of each issue for the past three months or so[8] to locate any changes that have not yet been incorporated into the *Official Compilation of Rules and Regulations of the State of Tennessee.*

TAR is also available on LexisNexis. To access it, select "Tennessee," then "Agency & Administrative Materials," then "TN – Tennessee Administrative Register." Alternatively, enter "Tennessee Administrative Register" as your search term in the "Find A Source" search box in LexisNexis. Be aware that the version of TAR presented on LexisNexis usually runs about a month behind the official version provided on the Secretary of State's website. Westlaw offers databases for tracking new and proposed regulations.[9] Keep in mind that the information contained in the Westlaw databases is usually not any more current than what can be found on the free Secretary of State's website, and is often significantly less current than the information on the Secretary of State's website.

D. Locate Agency Decisions and Case Opinions Interpreting and Applying the Regulation

Just as cases interpret and apply statutes, judicial and administrative decisions interpret and apply regulations. These decisions can

---

8. Usually new regulations and amendments are incorporated into the regulatory code within three months after their official adoption.

9. The database identifiers are TN-REGTRK, TN-REGTXT, and TN-REG-NET.

provide helpful context and insight to how a regulation may be applicable in your client's situation. However, finding agency and court decisions that interpret a regulation is usually more difficult than finding similar decisions for statutes. While statutes can be researched using an annotated code or a citation service such as KeyCite or Shepard's, Tennessee regulations are published in an *un*annotated code, and KeyCite and Shepard's do not provide citation services for them.

1. Agency Decisions

In addition to their rule-making function, agencies also act in a quasi-judicial role, adjudicating disputes pertaining to agency regulations or actions. There may be several layers of agency review, depending on the agency. Check with a particular agency to learn the procedure it follows.[10] The first level may involve a reviewer or adjudicator considering the claimant's file and making a recommendation or determination. Subsequently, a hearing may be held before an Administrative Law Judge (ALJ). These proceedings may resemble short, informal trials. At the conclusion of the hearing, the ALJ may issue a final order or a proposed order. If a party is dissatisfied with the decision of the ALJ, that party may appeal to the courts. Except in a few limited instances, appeal is taken to the Chancery Court.[11]

Some administrative decisions are available on LexisNexis and Westlaw. On LexisNexis, select Tennessee, then Cases, then Tennessee Cases, Administrative Decisions, and Attorney General Opinions Combined. This database includes decisions from the Department of Commerce and Insurance and from the Department of Revenue. Databases on Westlaw for Tennessee administrative decisions include TN-SECDEC (Tennessee Department of Commerce & Insurance Securities Division decisions), TNENV-ADMIN (Tennessee environ-

---

10. You may find this information on the agency's website, or you may need to call the agency and speak with someone there, such as a staff attorney or hearing officer's clerk.

11. Tenn. Code Ann. §4-5-322 (2005).

mental law administrative decisions), and TNWC-ADMIN (Tennessee workers' compensation administrative decisions).

In addition, a few selected administrative decisions are available online at www.law.utk.edu/ado/, but the vast majority are available only by visiting the office of the Secretary of State in Nashville, where they are compiled in the *Administrative Procedures Reports.*[12] Previously, some of the more notable administrative decisions were summarized and organized by topic in the *Administrative Law Digest.* This digest also included judicial opinions addressing administrative issues. Unfortunately, the *Administrative Law Digest* has not been updated or re-published since 1995. This digest is available online at www.state.tn.us/sos/apd/digest.pdf.

2. Case Opinions

Both law and chancery courts in Tennessee may hear matters involving the interpretation and application of regulations. Finding these cases can be challenging because, as noted above, there is no annotated regulatory code for Tennessee, and no electronic citator service to automatically retrieve cases that cite Tennessee regulations. You do have some options, though.

The *Administrative Law Digest* discussed above includes references to judicial decisions. This digest, compiled in 1995, is available at www.law.utk.edu/ado/. Tennessee cases on administrative law can also be found using the *West's Tennessee Digest 2d.* The "Administrative Law" topic includes headnotes from cases dealing with the organization, powers, and proceedings of administrative agencies, as well as judicial review and enforcement of administrative decisions. For cases that involve specific sub-areas of administrative law, check the corresponding topic in the digest. For example, headnotes from cases that interpret environmental regulations can be found in the "Environmental Law" topic.

Searching electronic databases of case law may also be an effective way to search for opinions that interpret a regulation. First, try

---

12. If you know the names of the parties, docket number, and date of decision, personnel at the Administrative Procedures Division of the Secretary of State may be able to copy and mail the decision to you, for a fee.

Table 6-4. Electronic Searches for Cases Interpreting Regulations

Search Phrase	Results in Westlaw TN-CS Database
1240-2-4-.04	176 cases
1240-2-4-.04(1)	87 cases
1240-2-4-.04 and ("private school" or tuition or "summer camp")	49 cases

searching a database of Tennessee case opinions using the regulation number (without sub-parts) as the search term. If the regulation you are researching is Tenn. Comp. R. & Regs. 1240-2-4-.03(1), start by using "1240-2-4-.03" as the search term.[13] If you retrieve very few results and believe there might be more cases out there, try broadening your search term by cutting off the final sub-part and adding a truncation character (e.g., "1240-2-4!"). If you retrieve too many results, consider putting in additional terms to ensure that the cases retrieved are relevant to the factual and legal issues you are researching. For example, if your issue has to do with when, under Tennessee child support regulations, a non-custodial parent can be required to purchase health insurance for his or her children, you might add search terms such as "insurance," "health," "medical," or "dental."

Table 6-4 shows possible searches to run on LexisNexis or Westlaw in order to retrieve cases on this issue: when can a non-custodial parent be required, under Tennessee child support regulations, to pay for summer camp expenses or private school tuition for his or her children? The Tennessee regulation dealing with "extraordinary education expenses" and "other extraordinary expenses" for children can be found at Tennessee Comp. R. & Regs. 1240-2-4-.04(1) *et seq.*

---

13. Exclude "Tenn. Comp. R. & Regs." from the search because sometimes citations in opinions are composed with minor variations in wording or punctuation, which could mean that the search would not retrieve otherwise relevant documents if your search phrase varied even slightly from what appeared in the document.

LexisNexis has a database of case opinions that deal with interpreting Tennessee regulations and with appeals from Tennessee administrative decisions. To locate this database, either enter "Tennessee Administrative Agency Cases" as a search phrase in the Find A Source search feature on LexisNexis, or select "Tennessee," then "Cases," then "By Area of Law," and then "TN Administrative Agency Cases." Westlaw has databases such as TNENV, which includes both case opinions and administrative agency decisions on environmental law. Using these types of specialized databases can help eliminate irrelevant results from your searches and thus save both time and money.

E. Contact Agency Personnel

The most valuable resource in administrative law research is often the agency itself. While statutes and regulations can be relatively easy to find, keep in mind that additional policies, guidelines, and decisions exist that may be difficult to access. Your research should include, where appropriate, talking to the agency's representatives to find out what material is available. For example, guidelines provided by the agency may outline steps to take and forms to use in applying for an occupational license or certification. Talking with agency representatives can provide valuable insight and guidance not available anywhere else.

IV. Attorney General Opinions

The Attorney General is the state's lawyer. In that role, the Attorney General provides opinions to the state that are similar to the advice of an attorney to a client.

The Attorney General provides opinions in response to specific questions posed by the Governor, an agency official, or a legislator. An agency director may ask whether a federal statute preempts a state statute in a particular matter, or a state senator may ask about the impact or possible interpretations of a statute if enacted. The Attorney General's responses to these questions are published online at www.attorneygeneral.state.tn.us/opyear.htm. To find an Attorney General opinion published between 1999 and the present, use the search box provided at that website, entering topical key words or the number of a statute or regulation that you are researching. You can also browse through the opinions by year. Attorney General opinions are numbered much like session laws: opinion 04-042 is the forty-second opinion released in 2004. Until 2000, Attorney General opinions were published primarily in print, under the title *Opinions of the Attorney General of Tennessee*. Using print resources to find an Attorney General opinion on a particular subject can be difficult, as they are organized chronologically and are not regularly indexed. Attorney General opinions on a particular statute are usually referenced in the annotations after that statute in the *Tennessee Code Annotated*. Attorney General opinions are also summarized and arranged using the topic and key number system in the *West's Tennessee Digest 2d*.

Recent Attorney General opinions are also available on Westlaw, LexisNexis, and other online legal research providers. To access them on Westlaw, use the database identifier TN-AG. On LexisNexis, select "Tennessee," then scroll down and under the heading "Agency and Administrative Materials," click on "TN Attorney General Opinions." Coverage starts in 1977 on both Westlaw and LexisNexis.

Most other states also publish opinions of their attorney general. As with Tennessee, many of these states make their recent opinions available online for free. You can find other states' Attorney General opinions on LexisNexis and Westlaw as well. Also, a complete set of formal attorney general opinions for all states, *State Attorney General Reports and Opinions*, is published in microfiche by the Hein company. If you are looking for an older opinion from another state, this microfiche set may be your best resource.

V. Federal Administrative Law

The federal government's agencies function much like Tennessee's. Federal agencies such as the Occupational Safety and Health Administration, the Internal Revenue Service, and the U.S. Fish and Wildlife Service are integral parts of the executive branch.

The federal administrative procedure act is codified at 5 U.S.C. § 551 *et seq.* Like Tennessee's administrative procedure act, its purpose is to promote uniformity, public participation, and public confidence in the fairness of the procedures used by agencies of the federal government.

A. *Code of Federal Regulations*

Federal regulations are published in the *Code of Federal Regulations,* which is usually referred to as the C.F.R. The C.F.R. is the codification of regulations issued by federal agencies. As with Tennessee's regulations, regulations in the C.F.R. are organized by agency and subject. The fifty numbered titles of the C.F.R. do not always correspond to the fifty numbered titles of the *United States Code,* although some topics do fall under the same title number in both codes. For instance, Title 7 in both the C.F.R. and the U.S.C. pertains to agriculture, but Title 11 in the U.S.C. addresses bankruptcy, while Title 11 in the C.F.R. deals with federal elections. See Table 6-5 for an example of a federal regulation.

C.F.R. volumes are re-published with changes and additions annually, with specific titles re-published in each quarter of the year. Titles 1 through 16 are re-published as of January 1[14]; Titles 17 through 27 are re-published as of April 1; Titles 28 through 41 are re-published as of July 1; and Titles 42 through 50 are re-published as of October 1. Realize, though, that the new volumes may not reach your library or be made available online until months after the schedule indicates. Each year, the covers of C.F.R. volumes are a different color, which makes it easy to tell whether a print volume has been re-published. If no changes were made in a particular volume for the new year, a cover with the new color is pasted on the old volume.

---

14. The exception is Title 3, "The President," which includes executive orders. Title 3 is re-published on a more irregular basis.

Table 6-5. Example of a Federal Regulation

---

21 C.F.R. § 102.54

TITLE 21 — FOOD AND DRUGS

CHAPTER I — DEPARTMENT OF HEALTH AND HUMAN SERVICES

SUBCHAPTER B — FOOD FOR HUMAN CONSUMPTION

PART 102 — COMMON OR USUAL NAME FOR NONSTANDARD-IZED FOODS

Subpart B — Requirements for Specific Nonstandardized Foods

Sec. 102.54. Seafood cocktails.

The common or usual name of a seafood cocktail in package form fabricated with one or more seafood ingredients shall be:

(a) When the cocktail contains only one seafood ingredient, the name of the seafood ingredient followed by the word "cocktail" (e.g. shrimp cocktail, crabmeat cocktail) and a statement of the percentage by weight of that seafood ingredient in the product in the manner set forth in § 102.5(b).

(b) When the cocktail contains more than one seafood ingredient, the term "seafood cocktail" and a statement of the percentage by weight of each seafood ingredient in the product in the manner set forth in § 102.5(b).

Source: *Code of Federal Regulations*, Title 21, Section 102.54 (2005).

To research a topic in the C.F.R., you may want to start with the general index. You can look up either your research terms or the agency's name. However, the general index is small and does not index the regulations in depth. Thus, using it can be frustrating and inefficient. It may be more efficient to begin your research in an annotated statutory code that contains references to related regulations for each statute. The *United States Code Service* tends to provide more references to regulations than does the *United States Code Annotated.* Another method that may help to find pertinent regulations is to start with an in depth, practice-oriented secondary source such as a looseleaf.[15] A good looseleaf will provide at least citations to important reg-

---

15. Subject-oriented looseleaf services are discussed in depth in Chapter 8.

ulations, while particularly thorough looseleafs may reprint relevant regulations in their entirety.

Federal regulations are available online at www.gpoaccess.gov/cfr/. While the text there is no more current than the print versions, a search feature is provided which may benefit those skilled in electronic research. LexisNexis, Westlaw, and other electronic legal research services provide searchable versions of the C.F.R. as well. Also, many federal agencies provide links from their web pages to separate databases containing just those agencies' regulations, rather than all regulations published by all agencies. If you are confident that you know which agency issued the regulations that apply to the situation you are researching, going directly to that agency's regulations is often easier and more efficient than trying to search the entire C.F.R.

B. *Federal Register*

New regulations and proposed changes to existing regulations are first published in the *Federal Register*, the federal equivalent of the *Tennessee Administrative Register*. The *Federal Register* is the first print source to publish regulations in their final form when they are adopted (i.e., before they are codified in the C.F.R.). In addition to providing the text of newly-adopted final regulations, the *Federal Register* also contains new proposed regulations and proposed amendments to regulations, responses to public comments on proposed regulations, notices of hearings, Presidential proclamations and other executive documents, and helpful tables and indexes. It is published almost every weekday, with continuous pagination throughout the year. This means that page numbers in the thousands are common.

The Government Printing Office provides a free, online version of the *Federal Register* at www.gpoaccess.gov/fr/. This site contains issues of the *Federal Register* going back to 1995. The *Federal Register* is also available on Westlaw, with back issues available from 1936,[16] and on LexisNexis, with back issues available from 1980.

---

16. On Westlaw, to access the full text of the *Federal Register* from 1936 to the present, use the FR-ALL database. *Federal Register* documents from

C. Updating Federal Regulations

To update a federal regulation in print or on the government's website, begin with the *List of C.F.R. Sections Affected* (the "L.S.A."). The *List of C.F.R. Sections Affected* is published monthly as a small booklet and is available as an online database at www.gpoaccess.gov/lsa/. As its name suggests, the L.S.A. lists all sections of the C.F.R. that have been affected by recent agency action. The L.S.A. provides page references to *Federal Register* issues where action affecting a section of the C.F.R. can be found.

Final updating in print requires reference to a table at the back of the *Federal Register* called "C.F.R. Parts Affected During [the current month]." Refer to this table in each *Federal Register* for the last day of each month for all the months between the most recent monthly L.S.A. issue and the current date. Also check the most recent issue of the *Federal Register* for the present month. The table contains more general information (whether a "part" has been affected, not a "section"), but will note changes made since the most recent L.S.A.

Final updating using the government's online sources requires using the *Current List of C.F.R. Parts Affected*. This list is updated daily and cumulates all C.F.R. parts changed since the publication of the most recent L.S.A. It is available at www.gpoaccess.gov/lsa/curlist.html. Federal regulations may also be updated using Shepard's (in paper or on LexisNexis) or KeyCite (on Westlaw).

D. Decisions of Federal Agencies

Like Tennessee agencies, federal agencies hold quasi-judicial hearings to decide disputes that arise under the agencies' regulations. Locating these decisions can be difficult, as each agency decides inde-

---

1936 through 1980 are displayed as .pdf images of the original printed pages rather than in the typical Westlaw format. Viewing these .pdf images may result in additional charges depending on the type of Westlaw subscription you are using. To access the full text of the *Federal Register* from 1981 to the present, use the FR database.

pendently whether, when, and how their decisions are published. Many agencies keep a rather erratic publication schedule. For citation purposes, you will want to locate the official source or reporter in which an agency publishes its decisions, if at all possible. Most of the official reporters are listed in the *Bluebook*, in Table T.1, under "United States official administrative publications." You may also be able to find federal administrative agency decisions on LexisNexis or Westlaw, as well as on an individual agency's web page. A list of individual agencies and a chart showing what types of documents, including opinions, each agency makes available on the Internet, can be found at www.washlaw.edu/doclaw/executive5m.html. This chart also provides direct links to the documents and opinions for each agency. Federal agency web pages may also provide helpful documents such as directories, organization charts, policy statements, and manuals for practice and proceedings before the agency.

Chapter 7

Citator Services

Before using any legal authority to analyze a problem, you must know how that authority has been treated by later actions of a court, legislature, or agency. A case may have been reversed or overruled; a statute may have been amended or repealed. Pocket parts in digests and annotated codes provide access to recent case opinions and statutes, but they do not tell you how the older authorities you have found have been treated. Ensuring that the cases, statutes, and other authorities you rely on represent the *current* law requires an additional step: updating your research using a citator service. This updating process is still sometimes referred to as "Shepardizing" because the first major updating tool was *Shepard's Citations.*

Checking to see whether your authorities are still good law is crucial, but it is not the only reason to use a citator service. You should also use citator services to expand your research by finding references to additional authorities addressing the same legal issues and to assist your own understanding of the prior and subsequent histories of the authorities you will rely on.

Citator services compile lists of citations to legal sources that have cited a particular authority. If you want to update a case opinion, for example, you could look up the citation to the case in *Shepard's Citations* in print, enter the citation in the Shepard's service on Lexis-Nexis, or enter the citation in the KeyCite service on Westlaw. Any of those citator services will then provide you with a list of authorities that cited your case, together with codes or symbols that tell you how your case was treated by those authorities. The online services also provide easy access to information about the prior and subsequent history of the case.

While updating online is easier and faster than in print, it is still a time-consuming activity, primarily because of the large number of sources you must read and analyze. But competent research requires updating, and your research is not finished until this step has been completed for each authority that you use in your legal analysis. Courts expect lawyers to update their research to ensure that their arguments are supported and to present the current state of the law in their filings. One federal court has noted that it is "really inexcusable" for any lawyer to fail to routinely use a citator service to update his or her work.[1] Failing to cite current law or disclose adverse authority may result in sanctions, malpractice suits, public embarrassment, and damage to your reputation, both within your firm and office and in the larger legal community. In one instance, a judge ordered a major law firm to copy for each of its partners and associates an opinion chastising the firm for failing to cite a case adverse to the client's argument.[2] In another case, an attorney was found to have willfully abused the judicial process and was ordered to pay over $14,000 in fees to the opposing party when he filed a complaint in reliance upon a case that was no longer good law. The court commented, when explaining its decision to impose the award of fees, that the attorney "never Shepardized his principle [sic] authority," and concluded with references to the attorney's "laziness, greed, [or] incompetence."[3]

I. Updating Online

To understand the process of updating an authority, you must be familiar with two basic terms. First, the authority you are updating, for example, a Tennessee case opinion, is called the *cited source* or

---

1. *Gosnell v. Rentokil, Inc.*, 175 F.R.D. 508, 510 (N.D. Ill. 1997).

2. *Golden Eagle Distrib. Corp. v. Burroughs Corp.*, 103 F.R.D. 124, 129 (N.D. Cal. 1984) ("For counsel to have been unaware of those cases means that they did not Shepardize their principal authority….").

3. *Taylor v. Belger Cartage Serv., Inc.*, 102 F.R.D. 172, 180–81 (W.D. Mo. 1984).

cited authority. Second, the authorities listed by a citator service are called *citing sources* or *citing references*.

There are several ways to get the updating process started using either Shepard's on LexisNexis or KeyCite on Westlaw. Additionally, both Shepard's and KeyCite offer a myriad of different options for customizing and displaying your results. Because those options change frequently, this book only covers the broadest basics of how to use those services. Current information and training materials on Shepard's and KeyCite are found on their respective web pages or from your school or firm's account representative.

A. Using Shepard's on LexisNexis

There are a number of different starting points for Shepard's on LexisNexis. You can Shepardize immediately by using a box on the front page of the LexisNexis service. You can also, after entering the "Research System" portion of LexisNexis, look for the tab for Shepard's. Alternatively, once you have pulled up a case opinion, statute, or other authority, you can Shepardize by clicking on the "Shepardize" link or on the Shepard's treatment symbol,[4] both of which appear toward the beginning of the page displaying the authority.

However you enter the Shepard's service, you will receive the same result: a list of citing sources. At the very top of the screen, you will see the name of your case, accompanied by the Shepard's treatment symbol assigned to it. Some of the more commonly seen symbols are explained in Table 7-1.

There are other treatment symbols as well. If you see a symbol that you do not recognize, or if you cannot remember exactly what a symbol means, hover your cursor over the symbol and a brief explanation will pop up.[5] Alternatively, look for the link to the "legend" that decodes the treatment symbols.

---

4. The Shepard's treatment symbol gives you an indication of how your case has been treated by later authorities.

5. Not all features mentioned here will work with all browsers. LexisNexis and Westlaw are designed so that all features will work with the latest ver-

Table 7-1. Shepard's Online Treatment Signals

Symbol	Meaning
Red octagon	Strong negative treatment or history of the case for at least one point of law.
Yellow triangle	Possible negative treatment or history of the case for at least one point of law.
Green diamond with plus sign inside	Positive treatment or history of the case for at least one point of law.

Although treatment symbols provide a quick insight into the potential validity of your cited source, you should never rely solely on the symbols and assume that you know how a cited source has been treated. For example, a case that addresses three completely different and unrelated points of law and has only one of those points overruled by a later case will always be marked with a red octagon, even if the other two points remain good law. So, it is crucial to read all the authorities citing your original source when those authorities indicate negative treatment, positive treatment, or any treatment directly related to your specific issue. Then you can make your own determination as to the validity and currency of your cited source.

Discerning which authorities in your list of Shepard's results to read takes some practice and familiarity with the system. At the top of your Shepard's results, you will see a gray, shaded box that summarizes the results. Just under the summary box, you will find links to prior history (the opinions generated in the same case prior to the decision of your cited source) and subsequent history (the opinions generated in the same case after the decision of your cited source, such as the opinion of a court that heard an appeal from your case). At least skimming through these opinions will help you understand the procedural posture of your case as well as its currency and validity.

---

sion of Internet Explorer, and researchers using other browsers may find that some functions do not work or display properly.

After the prior and subsequent history you will find a list of citing sources. When Shepardizing a case, citing sources will often be case opinions that have cited your case. In Shepard's, those citing sources are organized by jurisdiction—for example, citing sources from the Sixth Circuit will be listed together. You will also see a description of how each citing source treated the cited source—"cited by," "followed by," "criticized by," and so on. If you do not know what one of the indications means, click on the indication itself (the words "followed by," for instance) and a pop-up box will display the definition for you. Again, it is critical that you actually read the citing sources to make your own determination of how they treated your cited source.

After case opinions, you will typically find links to other kinds of citing authorities such as law review articles, treatises, and legal encyclopedias that have cited your authority. These authorities will be hyperlinked for you. Skimming through these secondary citing sources can be an excellent way to find materials that further explain the area of law for you and allow you to mine for additional citations to relevant authorities.

A series of links toward the top of the Shepard's page allows you to customize your results. This is especially helpful when dealing with cited sources that have been cited dozens or hundreds of times. You can choose to look at only authorities that treat your cited source positively or negatively. You can also focus on citing sources from a particular jurisdiction, citing sources that address the same point of law contained in a particular headnote from your cited source, or citing sources that contain a particular search term. Which citing sources you want to read in depth, which to skim over briefly, and whether to entirely ignore any of the citing sources will depend on how many citing sources there are to begin with, your purpose in Shepardizing, and the amount of time and money you and your client feel is reasonable to devote to Shepardizing. As a general rule, when faced with many citing sources, you should consider following the steps in Table 7-2. Although these steps are primarily applicable to updating case law, many are also transferable to updating statutes and other authorities as well.

After you Shepardize initially, you may want to consider setting up a Shepard's Alert. Shepard's Alert will automatically search for new

Table 7-2. Reading Citing Sources on Shepard's

1. Scrutinize links to prior and subsequent appellate history. If you do not already have a thorough understanding of the history, read the opinions linked and outline the history for yourself.

2. Write down the headnote numbers of the headnotes in your cited case that relate to the points of law you are particularly interested in, and note particular search terms or phrases that appear in your cited case that are likely to also appear in citing sources that address your issues or facts.

3. Look at all cases from your jurisdiction that have negatively treated your cited case. Skim through each negatively-treating case and make a determination as to whether the negative treatment has to do with your particular legal issue. For any citing authority that deals with your issue negatively, read the authority thoroughly and carefully.

4. Next, look at all citing cases from your jurisdiction that have positively or neutrally treated your cited case. Again, skim through these cases and find the ones that deal with your particular legal issue. These positive cases may be even more beneficial to your client's position than the cited authority you started with.

5. Skim citing cases from other jurisdictions that address your issue. You may need to read and analyze them in depth in some circumstances (for instance, if all of the cases from your jurisdiction are very old, and newer cases from other jurisdictions indicate a growing movement either to strongly affirm or to overrule your cited case's holding).

6. Skim through citing secondary sources to see if any of them appear to be particularly helpful to you in your research process. Consider reading them to gain further understanding of the issues or to find more citations to relevant authorities.

7. Use the Table of Authorities feature to check the strength of your cited case. The Table of Authorities will show you the subsequent treatment of cases that your case relies upon. For example, say your case, *Gold v. Silver*, relied heavily upon *Dog v. Cat* in reaching its legal conclusions. A later case, *Sky v. Ocean*, expressly overruled *Dog v. Cat* but did not mention *Gold v. Silver* in the text of the opinion. In effect, *Sky v. Ocean* has cast very strong doubt on the validity and currency of *Gold v. Silver*, but has done so in a way that would likely not be reflected in a basic Shepard's search. Using the Table of Authorities link will allow you to Shepardize the cases relied upon in *Gold v. Silver* to help you find any otherwise hidden weaknesses in its validity.

Table 7-3. KeyCite Treatment Symbols

Symbol	Meaning
Red flag	No longer good for at least one point of law.
Yellow flag	Some negative history but not overruled.
Blue "H"	Case has some history.

citing sources on a regular basis and email you the results. Since legal research, analysis, and writing on a given project can be an ongoing process lasting months or even years, you will want to periodically update again to see if important new authorities have cited your case. Setting up a Shepard's Alert is one way to ensure that this process takes place and does not slip your mind.

B. Using KeyCite on Westlaw

Just as with Shepard's, there are a number of different entry points to KeyCite on Westlaw. You can enter a citation in a small text box on the Westlaw law school home page, look for the "KeyCite" link on any page in the Westlaw research system, or follow links from your retrieved documents. Clickable treatment symbols, like those in Shepard's, will appear on Westlaw documents. Although the symbols do vary from the symbols used in Shepard's, the theory is the same. Some of the more commonly-seen treatment symbols on Westlaw appear in Table 7-3.

If you see a treatment symbol that you do not understand, look at the frame on the left-hand side of the page for an explanation of the symbol, or click on the "KeyCite" link at the top of the page to find more information.

Another way to go directly to KeyCite results from your cited source is to use the hyperlinks in the left-hand side of the page displaying your cited source. Typically, with cases, the main text of the case opinion on Westlaw is set out in the frame on the right-hand side of the page. A narrower frame on the left-hand side contains links related to the case. Look in the left-hand frame for links to the case's

"Full History," "Direct History—Graphical View," and "Citing References." All of these hyperlinks are shortcuts into the KeyCite system.

The Full History on KeyCite includes links to all of the prior and subsequent decisions generated in your case. This full history can be helpful in understanding the procedural posture of your case, as well as its precedential value. The Full History page will also include links to briefs, motions, transcripts of oral arguments, and other court filings from your case that are available on Westlaw. Reading the briefs of the parties that were filed in a trial or hearing that resulted in your court decision can be tremendously enlightening—but also time consuming, so consider carefully whether reading them is appropriate.

Some researchers prefer to look at the history of their cited case in a graphical, flow-chart format rather than piecing it together through the list of citations generated by the Full History link. If you tend to be a more visually-oriented person, the Direct History—Graphical View link may be preferable to Full History. Clicking that link will generate a flow chart showing the evolution of your cited case, and providing links to any prior and subsequent decisions that are available on Westlaw.

The "Citing References" link will generate a list of all authorities on Westlaw that have referenced your cited case. First, a note of caution: the citing authorities on the list will have KeyCite treatment symbols next to them. Those symbols refer to how each of those citing authorities have been treated by later cases, not how they treat your cited authority. It is very easy for someone unfamiliar with KeyCite to come to an erroneous conclusion with these symbols. Suppose the cited case that you are updating is *Blue v. Green*. You click on Citing References to generate a list of citing authorities, and see that the first authority listed is *Smith v. Jones*, which has a red flag next to it. That does not mean that *Smith v. Jones* overruled *Blue v. Green*. It means that *Smith v. Jones* itself was overruled on at least one point of law.

On the "Citing References" page, KeyCite places negative references first. Among cases that treated your cited source negatively, those that are judged to discuss it in the most depth are listed first, and those that only mention your cited source briefly are listed later. KeyCite uses a star system to indicate the depth with which each citing authority discusses the cited authority. Four stars means that the citing authority discusses your cited authority for more than a page, while one star means that your cited authority was only mentioned briefly, usually in a string citation.

After the negative cases, you will find the positive cases, again arranged by depth of treatment of your cited authority. The list of citing sources will also contain notations showing which of the West headnotes from your cited authority each citing authority relates to. You can scan the list of citing sources looking for the headnote numbers relating to your particular legal issue, so that you know which citing sources you should spend your time reviewing in depth.

The citing sources on KeyCite may include case opinions, law review articles, treatises, Attorney General opinions, and appellate and trial court briefs and documents that are available on Westlaw. If you have many results in your list of citing sources, you may want to limit your displayed results by jurisdiction, date, headnotes, type of citing source, depth of treatment,[6] or search terms included in the citing sources (in KeyCite, the feature that allows you to narrow results by adding an additional search term is called "Locate"). If you want to have KeyCite automatically check for new citations and email you the results on a periodic basis, look for the "KeyCite Alert" link.

II. Updating with Citators in Print

Shepard's in print is by far the most commonly-used print citator. It is the source of the legal jargon that refers to the general process of updating with any citator service: *Shepardizing.* Shepardizing in print

---

6. Limiting your results by depth of treatment is a very useful feature. Restricting the results so that you are only shown citing authorities that discuss the cited authority for more than a paragraph or page speeds up your research process by allowing you to focus on authorities that deal with your issue in depth. Limiting results by depth of treatment is a feature currently available on Westlaw only. Shepard's on LexisNexis does not sort results by depth of treatment or give any indication of depth of treatment.

takes longer than using either Shepard's on LexisNexis or KeyCite on Westlaw, and the print citators are not nearly as current as those available online. However, Shepardizing in print may be the only option at some point in your legal research career.

To Shepardize in print, the researcher first locates the correct set of Shepard's volumes. Shepard's publishes different series of citator volumes corresponding to different reporters. A cited authority published in the *Federal Reporter* should be researched in the *Shepard's Federal Citations*, while a cited authority published in the *South Western Reporter* should be researched in *Shepard's Southwestern Reporter Citations* or in the citator set corresponding to the state of the cited authority, such as *Shepard's Tennessee Citations*.

Once you locate the correct set, you must make sure you have all applicable bound volumes and softbound supplements. The easiest way to do that is to locate the most recent supplement by checking the dates on the front cover. The most recent supplement has usually been published within the past six weeks. If you cannot find a supplement published in that time frame, ask a librarian for assistance, as it may mean that a supplemental volume has been misplaced or was not received. Once you have the most recent supplement, look on the front cover for the list of "What Your Library Should Contain." This list will include the dates of all the supplements and bound volumes you will need to check. It is not unusual to have to check five or six volumes and supplements to completely update a cited authority using in Shepard's in print.

Once you have assembled all the volumes that you need, you should arrange them in chronological order and either work from oldest to most recent, or vice-versa. Cited sources are arranged in numerical order by citation,[7] and after each cited source comes a list of citing sources. Because space in the print version of Shepard's is lim-

---

7. Remember to be careful with series numbers. Cases from the *Federal Reporter, 2nd Series* will be in a different portion of a Shepard's volume than the *Federal Reporter* or the *Federal Reporter, 3rd Series*. In fact, they may be in different volumes entirely. The name of the reporter and its series are at the top of every page in each Shepard's volume.

ited, these citations are extremely abbreviated. You will also see alphabetic codes indicating how the citing sources treated the citing source. For example, a citing source with a small "o" next to it overruled the cited source. Legends that explain all of the citation and treatment abbreviations can be found at either the front or back of each Shepard's volume or supplement. In addition, each print volume of Shepard's has a sample page with explanations of each component of the entries for one authority.

III. The Process of Updating

As you read the citing sources gathered in your updating process, decide whether they address the legal question at issue in your client's problem. If a citing source that treats your cited authority negatively analyzes only points that are not relevant to your client's situation, make a note of that fact and move on.[8] If the citing source is neutral or positive but irrelevant to your client's specific legal issue, disregard the citing source and move to the next one.

If a source is on point, analyze its impact on your case. Does this new source change the rule announced in your case, either by reversing or overruling it? Does it follow your case by stating the rule and applying it to a similar fact pattern? Does the new source distinguish or criticize your case? If so, how and why?

Reading the sources you found in your Shepard's search not only will help determine whether your initial cited authority is still "good law," but also may lead you to cases in which the court's reasoning is explained more fully or to cases with facts more similar to yours.

As you expand the universe of cases that are on point for your issue, look for trends in frequency and treatment of case citations. In

---

8. Although you will not usually have to deal with these types of sources again, you will want to have a record of why a negative citing source is irrelevant to your client's legal situation, in case the opposing counsel or another attorney in your firm questions the validity of the authority that you cite.

general, cases that have been cited frequently and followed extensively should form the basis of your analysis, if such cases are available. A case that has been ignored in later opinions may be excluded or relegated to a position of lesser importance in your analysis unless the facts are very similar to yours or the reasoning is especially relevant. A line of cases that criticize or distinguish your case will have to be countered in your analysis.

A. When to Update

Citators can be a valuable research tool at several points in the research process. Some lawyers update cases as soon as they find them. A lawyer following this method knows immediately whether a case is still respected authority, instead of wasting valuable time analyzing a case opinion that has already been overruled. At the same time, the lawyer also finds other cases and secondary sources that discuss the same points of law as the first case.

Other lawyers Shepardize cases later in the research process. In this instance, the lawyer would begin by finding cases in annotated codes or digests, or by searching online databases. The lawyer would then read the cases, begin to outline an argument, and update only the cases that will likely appear in the memorandum. This lawyer will have to update fewer cases, but may have started to develop a line of analysis that is no longer "good law." In this case, the lawyer may need to do additional research or may need to rethink the argument. Moreover, this lawyer will not be using a citator as a research tool for finding additional cases and secondary sources, which is one of its best functions.

As lawyers move to doing researching primarily online, the risk of waiting to update cases has been lessened. Many lawyers now follow a practice that blends the two strategies of updating immediately, as cases are found, and updating at a significantly later point in their research. What lawyers can do now is find cases online, and immediately update those that are flagged with negative treatment symbols.[9]

---

9. Remember that a negative treatment symbol does not necessarily mean the cited case has received any negative treatment whatsoever with re-

Then they wait until later to update cases with positive or no treatment signals. This approach minimizes the risk of unwittingly using bad case law to develop your argument, although it still does not allow the lawyer to make full use of the citator as a method for doing additional research and finding more "good" authorities.

B. Updating Other Authorities

While this chapter has focused on using citator services to update a case opinion, remember that many authorities can be updated. Statutes, constitutional provisions, Attorney General opinions, regulations, court rules, jury instructions, and a number of secondary sources can all be updated using the various citator services. If you are working online, look for the link to Shepard's on LexisNexis or KeyCite on Westlaw from your authority.

If you are signing on to Westlaw or LexisNexis just to update with KeyCite or Shepard's, be sure that you know the correct format for the citation to your source to enter into the citator. If you accidentally put in the wrong format and Shepard's or KeyCite runs a search for the wrong source, you will still be charged for your result.[10] If you are unsure of the correct format for your citation, look for the "Publications List" link on Westlaw or the "Citations Format" link on LexisNexis.

---

spect to your particular legal issue. In many instances an online case with a red flag or red octagon is a perfectly good precedent on a given point of law.

10. The current basic price for running one Shepard's or KeyCite search is about six dollars per cited authority, though many firms negotiate different pricing levels or packages.

Chapter 8

Secondary Sources

Other people have previously researched and analyzed many of the legal issues you will encounter in law school and in law practice. Many have published their work in legal encyclopedias, treatises, law review articles, practice handbooks, and other secondary sources. These sources are "secondary" because they are commentary that is written *about* the law. In contrast, "primary" authority is written by legislatures, courts, and administrative agencies, and it *is* the law.

Lawyers use secondary sources to learn about the law and to find references to primary authorities. Often, beginning a new research project with secondary sources will be more effective than beginning immediately to search for statutes, cases, or regulations on point. This is particularly true if you are exploring an area of law that is new to you. By locating and understanding secondary sources on point, you can more easily analyze the issues involved in your client's problem and more quickly find pertinent primary authorities. The text of a good secondary source will explain terminology and concepts unfamiliar to you. It may suggest causes of action or defenses that had not yet occurred to you. It can explain the development of a field of law over time and help you see how your issue fits into a larger framework. This understanding will make it possible for you to develop a more effective list of research terms. It will help you understand the case opinions, statutes, and regulations when you read them. In addition, secondary sources often provide a shortcut to researching primary authority by including numerous references to case opinions, statutes, and regulations, and explaining why these authorities may be important to the issue you are researching.

This chapter covers legal encyclopedias, treatises and other books, forms, jury instructions, legal periodicals (including law reviews and bar journals), *American Law Reports* (a hybrid commentary-reporter, most often consulted for its commentary), topical looseleaf services, restatements, and uniform laws and model codes.[1] The chapter concludes with a discussion of when and how to use secondary sources in your research.

Some secondary sources reprint selected primary authority, so, despite the title of this chapter, some primary authorities are covered here. For example, *American Law Reports* volumes include the full text of some judicial opinions as well as commentary on those opinions. Topical looseleaf services (also sometimes called mini-libraries) are valuable because they may contain, in one setting, statutes, regulations, and judicial and administrative opinions, as well as commentary.

The process for researching secondary sources varies depending on the source. A general outline for using paper-based sources is provided in Table 8-1.

I. Legal Encyclopedias

Legal encyclopedias will look and function like other, more general print encyclopedias that may you have used in the past, such as the *Encyclopedia Britannica*. Legal encyclopedias provide basic information on a wide variety of legal subjects. Just as with general encyclopedias, those subjects are called *topics* and are arranged alphabetically within the bound encyclopedia volumes. Many states have their

---

1. Because there are so many of them, this chapter cannot include a comprehensive list of all Tennessee practice and secondary materials. For reference to books and newsletters in specific areas of law, see *Tennessee Practice Materials*, provided by the University of Tennessee College of Law Library, available at: www.law.utk.edu/library/tnlaw.htm.

Table 8-1. Outline for Researching Secondary Sources in Paper

1. Generate a list of research terms.

2. Search your library's catalog for the location of relevant secondary sources or ask a librarian to help you locate the best secondary sources.

3. Search the index of the secondary source.

4. Find the relevant portion of the main volume. Reading the commentary will help your comprehension of the legal issues. Within the commentary, often in footnotes, you will find references to primary authority.

5. Check for pocket parts or supplements to the secondary authority to make sure that you are reading the most current information it provides.

6. Read, analyze, and update the primary authorities you found cited in the secondary authority.

own encyclopedias. Tennessee's is *Tennessee Jurisprudence.* The two national legal encyclopedias are *Corpus Juris Secundum* (C.J.S.) and *American Jurisprudence, Second Edition* (Am. Jur. 2d).

To use an encyclopedia, review its softbound index volumes, usually shelved at the end of the set, for your research terms. The references will include both an abbreviated word or phrase that identifies the topic and a section number.[2] Alternatively, there may be an instruction to "see [alternative topic], this volume" or "see [alternative topic], this series." This instruction means to look up that alternative topic in the index rather than the research term you used. The encyclopedia's topic abbreviations are explained in tables in the front of each index volume. The spine of each of the main encyclopedia volumes shows the alphabetic range of topics included in that volume. For example, the topic "Contracts" would be included in a volume

---

2. Do not confuse the section number with a volume or page number.

with Constitutional Law—Correctional Law on the spine. The spine will not list each and every topic included in the volume. It will just show the alphabetic range of topics.

Next, skim the material at the beginning of that topic for an overview and general information. Then turn to the particular section given in the index and read the text there. The text of most encyclopedia entries is cursory because the goal of the writers is to summarize the law rather than to analyze it in great depth. Entries in national encyclopedias will identify major variations that exist between different jurisdictions, but they do not attempt to resolve differences or recommend improvements in the law.

The footnotes that accompany the text in an encyclopedia are usually just as helpful as the text, if not more so. The footnotes will usually cite directly to primary authorities, such as case opinions and statutes, that support the commentary in the discussion. Because finding and citing primary authorities is almost always the ultimate goal of any legal researcher, using these footnotes as a springboard to further research in primary authorities is often an efficient way to begin your research.

In *Tennessee Jurisprudence*, those footnotes will generally refer to Tennessee authorities that uphold and apply the principles discussed in the text. In a national encyclopedia, the citations to authorities could be from any, or many, states. You can still use those citations to find Tennessee cases addressing the same principles, though. One way to do this is to look up the cases from another jurisdiction in a West reporter or on Westlaw, note the West topic and key number, and then look up that topic and key number in *West's Tennessee Digest 2d* to locate similar Tennessee cases. As with virtually all other legal research, you must check the pocket parts of encyclopedias to find references to the most recent authorities and commentary.

Encyclopedias are also available on Westlaw and LexisNexis. On Westlaw, *Corpus Juris Secundum* can be found with the database identifier CJS, and *American Jurisprudence* with the database identifier AMJUR. *Tennessee Jurisprudence* is not available on Westlaw. On LexisNexis, *Tennessee Jurisprudence* can be searched by selecting "Tennessee," then Treatises & Analytical Materials, then Tennessee Jurisprudence. *American Jurisprudence* can be found by looking under the main "Legal" tab for the heading "Secondary Legal," selecting Jurisprudence & ALR, and then clicking American Jurisprudence 2d. *Corpus Juris Secundum* is not available on LexisNexis.

II. Treatises and Other Books

A book on a legal topic can provide a deeper discussion and more relevant references than might be found in an encyclopedia entry. Legal texts include treatises, hornbooks, nutshells, practice guides, form books, and continuing legal education materials. All of these books share the purpose of covering a single legal topic, such as contracts or admiralty law, or a single jurisdiction, such as Tennessee. They are distinguished from each other by their depth of coverage and the audience to whom they are directed.

A. Academic Works

Treatises, hornbooks, and nutshells are most frequently written for and used by law students and law professors. Treatises are generally considered to be more comprehensive than hornbooks, which offer a more summarized view of a particular area of law. Nutshells are a series of books published by West that offer an even more condensed explanation of the law than hornbooks. They tend to be most frequently used by law students and members of the general public seeking an introduction to a particular area of law. Treatises, hornbooks, and nutshells are typically national in scope rather than focused on one particular state.

To find a treatise or other book addressing your topic, search your law library's catalog or ask a law librarian for recommendations. If searching the catalog, try searching by key word if possible. If you want to find a book that is devoted to your jurisdiction, include the name of your state as a key word in your search. For example, searching the key words "Tennessee and wills and estates" in most law library catalogs will give you a reference to the well-respected work,

Pritchard on the Law of Wills and Administration of Estates: Embracing the Law and Practice in Tennessee. Some libraries, especially academic libraries, house their hornbooks and nutshells in special collections apart from the main shelves. Since these works are popular with law students, they may be kept on reserve or placed in an easily accessible and visible location. To find a nutshell in your library, start by doing a key word search in the library catalog using a word or two that might be in the title combined with the word "nutshell." Because the books in the nutshell series all contain the word "nutshell" in the title (such as *Criminal Procedure in a Nutshell*), this type of search should retrieve a nutshell on the subject you are studying if it is in the library's collection.

To use a treatise or other book, begin with either the table of contents or the index. In multi-volume treatises, the index is usually in the last volume of the series. Locate your research terms and record the references given. A reference will be to a page number, section number, or paragraph number, depending on the publisher. Turn to that part of the book, read the text, and note any pertinent authorities cited in the footnotes.

Some treatises are so well known and widely respected that a colleague or supervisor may suggest that you begin research with a particular title. Examples include Tribe's *American Constitutional Law*, *Powell on Real Property*, Wright & Miller's *Federal Practice and Procedure*, and *Moore's Federal Practice*. Table 8-2 includes a sample page from a well-known treatise.

B. Continuing Legal Education Materials and Other Works for Practitioners

Practice guides, form books, jury instructions, and continuing legal education materials are most often used by lawyers; however, they can be valuable resources for legal academics and the general public as well. These works are more likely than academic works to be directed toward a specific jurisdiction rather than attempting to cover a national scope of authorities.

Table 8-2. Excerpt from Wright & Miller's
Federal Practice and Procedure

A. GENERAL FEDERAL QUESTION
JURISDICTION

3561. Federal Question Jurisdiction—In General.

3561.1 Amount in Controversy.

3562. The Meaning of "Arising Under."

3563. "Constitution, Laws, or Treaties of the United States."

3564. Substantiality of the Federal Question.

3565. "Protective Jurisdiction."

3566. Determination From the Well-Pleaded Complaint.

3567. Pendent Jurisdiction—The Background.

3567.1 Application of the Present Rule.

3567.2 Pendent Parties.

---

§3561. Federal Question Jurisdiction—In General

The Constitution provides that federal courts may be given jurisdiction over "Cases, in Law and Equity, arising under this Constitution, the Laws of the United States, and Treaties made, or which shall be made, under their authority."[1] Cases that fall under this head of jurisdiction usually are spoken of as involving a "federal question."[2]

1. Constitution U.S. Const., Art. III, §2. **2. "Federal question"** E.g., Thurston Motor Lines, Inc. v. Jordan K. Rand, Ltd., 1983, 103 S.Ct. 1343, 1344, 460 U.S. 533, ___, 75 L.Ed.2d 260. E.g., Steffel v. Thompson, 1974, 94 S.Ct. 1209, 1218, 415 U.S. 452, 464, 39 L.Ed.2d 505. Oneida Indian Nation v. County of Oneida, 1974, 94 S.Ct. 772, 776, 785, 414 U.S. 661, 39 L.Ed.2d 73.	American Law Institute, Study of Division of Jurisdiction between State and Federal Courts, Official Draft, 1969, p. 162. See also §3562 n. 4. Compare, however, London, "Federal Question" Jurisdiction—A Snare and a Delusion, 1959, 57 Mich.L. Rev. 835.

Source: 13B Charles Alan Wright & Arthur R. Miller, *Federal Practice and Procedure* § 3561 (2d ed 1984). Reprinted with permission of West, a Thomson business.

1. Practice Guides

Practice guides are intended to assist attorneys in a particular field of law. These guides generally consist of straightforward explanations of the law, references to related authorities, and directions for proceeding in specific types of actions. Practice guides may also include checklists of steps to take or sample forms to use in preparing transactional documents or court filings. Often practice guides are published in paperback and are reissued every year or two rather than being updated by pocket parts or looseleaf inserts.

Within each jurisdiction, a few works may be so widely used and highly thought of that they are cited and referenced almost as if they were mandatory authorities. These works are often referred to in practice just by the name of the author or by a shortened title, which may be confusing for a new legal researcher. Examples of these well known works in Tennessee include *Pritchard on the Law of Wills and Administration of Estates: Embracing the Law and Practice in Tennessee* (often simply called "Pritchard"), and Cohen et al.'s *Tennessee Law of Evidence.*[3]

2. Form Books

Form books consist primarily of sample forms to be adapted by attorneys or *pro se* litigants, but may include some summarized explanations of the law or guidance for attorneys using them. A form can be a great shortcut in drafting a legal document, such as a complaint or a lease agreement, especially for someone drafting that type of document for the first time in an unfamiliar area of law. A form can provide an excellent starting point by keeping you from reinventing the wheel.

Take care in using any form. Forms are designed for general circumstances, not for your particular client's situation. Before using a form, make sure that you understand every word in the form and modify the form to suit your client's needs. Do not simply fill in the

3. The Pritchard and Cohen works were cited by Tennessee appellate courts over 300 times between 2001 and 2006.

blanks and assume that the form correctly represents your client's position. Unless a particular form is prescribed or approved by a statute or by the court,[4] you may want to revise the wording to eliminate unnecessary "legalese"—standard legal jargon that has traditionally been added to legal documents, making them harder to understand than may be necessary.

Forms are available in diverse sources. Some form books may be geared towards a particular jurisdiction. For example, Tennessee has several general-purpose form sets, such as *Gore's Forms for Tennessee Annotated*, Robinson's *Tennessee Forms*, and Leveille's two sets, *Tennessee Legal and Business Forms* and *Litigation Forms and Analysis*. Other form books may be directed toward a specific area of law and are more likely to be national in scope rather than focused on one state such as Tennessee. *Fletcher Corporate Forms Annotated* is one of many sets of business forms intended for a national audience.

There are also many form books that cover a broad range of topics and jurisdictions. Well-known federal form book sets include *West's Federal Forms* and *Bender's Federal Practice Forms*. National form book sets that are common in law libraries include *American Jurisprudence Legal Forms 2d* and *Nichols Cyclopedia of Legal Forms Annotated*.

To find forms or a form book, search the library catalog by key word, including the name of your topic or jurisdiction and the word "forms." You may also ask a law librarian for a recommendation of the form books most often used in the area you are researching. Practice guides and continuing legal education materials may also include forms, so it may be worthwhile to search those sources. Many form series, both those national and local in scope, are available in a searchable format on either LexisNexis or Westlaw.

3. Jury Instructions

Pattern jury instructions are form jury instructions often used by lawyers, judges, and their clerks who have been charged with draft-

---

4. For example, Tennessee Rule of Appellate Procedure 48 approves the use of the forms set out in an appendix to the Rules.

ing instructions for use at the end of a trial. The drafters of pattern jury instructions attempt to provide succinct statements of all of the elements of a cause of action, or of the basis for damages or a particular defense. Thus, pattern jury instructions are also quite useful to lawyers who are marshaling their facts and arguments in preparation for trial. Jury instructions are also useful to legal researchers who would like a quick introduction to settled law on a particular issue in their jurisdiction. Pattern jury instructions typically include references to the primary authorities from which they were derived: for example, the pertinent parts of the *Tennessee Code Annotated* and important case opinions that set out the elements of a particular cause of action or defense.

The Tennessee Judicial Conference has committees on pattern jury instructions for both criminal and civil matters. Their publications, *Tennessee Pattern Jury Instructions-Criminal* and *Tennessee Pattern Jury Instructions-Civil*, are contained in volumes 7 and 8, respectively, of the set *Tennessee Practice*. In addition, *Tennessee Pattern Jury Instructions-Civil* is published as a separate looseleaf set by the Tennessee Judicial Conference. These sets are referred to by Tennessee lawyers and judges by their initials: T.P.I.-Civil and T.P.I-Criminal. The pattern jury instructions are not mandatory. As the preface to the civil set notes, "they are offered merely as a guide, not a straitjacket."

Many of the federal circuits also prepare and publish pattern jury instructions for use in that circuit. Some circuits publish only criminal or civil jury instructions, while others publish both. The Sixth Circuit, to which Tennessee belongs, has published its own *Pattern Criminal Jury Instructions* for use in criminal trials. Try searching your law library catalog for the subject "Instructions to Juries United States" to see if your law library holds jury instructions for the circuit you are researching. Also, many circuits are publishing their pattern jury instructions on the Internet. The Sixth Circuit's Pattern Criminal Jury Instructions can be found at www.ca6.uscourts.gov/Internet/crim _jury_insts.htm.

Pattern jury instructions are also drafted and published on a national basis for specific areas of law. These may be drafted for publication by a commercial publisher, or they may be prepared by a national organization such as the American Bar Association. Again, these types of model jury instructions may be useful to a legal researcher looking for a succinct introduction to an area of law. Some looseleaf sets may contain pattern jury instructions, or you may find them in a separate work, such as Loring's *Model Jury Instructions: Patent Litigation.*

4. Continuing Legal Education Materials

Attorneys in Tennessee are required to attend continuing legal education (CLE) courses periodically to maintain their membership in the state's bar. Topics range from writing better briefs to the latest updates in eminent domain law in Tennessee. While some CLE classes are aimed at new lawyers just learning the building blocks of practice, many CLE courses are intended to offer new insights on cutting-edge legal issues. A CLE course may be led by practitioners, judges, or law professors.

Frequently, the person or organization presenting the course prepares handouts that include outlines of the topics covered, sample forms, checklists, and explanations. These handouts may be compiled, bound, and published. While they can provide much valuable information, and can be particularly helpful when researching the law specific to Tennessee, they do have drawbacks. They usually do not have indexes, and since they are not supplemented, they tend to go out of date quickly.

The largest publisher of Tennessee CLE materials is the National Business Institute (NBI). Many of NBI's more popular courses are repeated each year, meaning that a new volume of materials on the same topic is published annually. When researching using CLE materials, make sure that you have the most recently published volume on your topic. Large publishers of CLE material that is national in scope include the Practising Law Institute (PLI) and the American Law Institute, in conjunction with the American Bar Association (ALI-ABA).

One way to locate CLE materials is to search the library catalog by author, using the name of a CLE publisher as the author. NBI, PLI and ALI-ABA materials are also available in searchable electronic format. Selected ALI-ABA and PLI materials are available on Westlaw,[5] and some ALI-ABA materials can be found on LexisNexis.[6] Selected materials from the National Business Institute's Tennessee series are available on Westlaw.[7]

III. Legal Periodicals

A. Law Reviews and Journals

Law reviews and law journals publish scholarly articles written by law professors, judges, attorneys, and law students. Each article explores a specific legal issue in great detail. Freed from the constraints of representing a client's interests or deciding a particular case, an author is able to explore whether the laws currently in force are the best legal rules and to propose changes.

Reading articles published in law reviews and journals can provide a thorough understanding of current law because the authors often explain the existing and historical law before making their recommendations for the future. These articles may also identify weaknesses or new trends in the law that might be relevant to your client's situation. As with encyclopedias, the many footnotes in law review and law journal articles can provide an excellent entry point for locating relevant primary authorities. When dealing with "cutting edge" legal issues, however, there may not be much, or any, primary authority on point. Law review articles may be especially persuasive then. They will also point to primary authorities that may be used to support your arguments because they uphold analogous or related principles of law.

---

5. To find these materials, go to the Westlaw Directory and follow the links through the "Practice Guides and CLE Materials" menu.

6. From the main "Legal" menu, go to the "Secondary Legal" subheading, then select "CLE Materials."

7. Database identifiers include NBI-TNBUS (Tennessee business law), NBI-TNFL (Tennessee family law), NBI-TNRP (Tennessee real property law), and NBI-TNEPP (Tennessee estate planning and probate law).

Articles written by students are called "Notes" or "Comments." Although usually considered not as authoritative as articles written by professors, judges, or attorneys, student articles can provide clear and careful analysis and their footnotes can be valuable research tools.[8] Shorter law review pieces, also generally written by students, summarize a recent case that the publication's editors consider important. These are called "Case Notes" or "Recent Developments." They notify readers of important developments in the law but do not analyze or critique the case in depth.

Law reviews and law journals are generally published by students who were selected through a competition for membership or according to their grades. Each law school typically has one general-interest law review that covers a broad range of topics. Examples include the *Tennessee Law Review*, the *Vanderbilt Law Review*, and the *University of Memphis Law Review*. Most law schools also publish other law journals that focus on a specific area of law, for example, the *Vanderbilt Journal of Transnational Law* and the *DePaul Journal of Health Care Law*. Table 8-3 lists law reviews and journals published by Tennessee law schools.

Law reviews and journals are published first in softcover booklets. Later, several issues will be bound into a single volume. Articles are located by the volume number, the name of the journal, and the first page of the article. Law review articles are also available online. How to access them is described in section IIIC of this chapter.

Law review and law journal articles are not kept up-to-date with revisions or supplements, but you can find out whether an article has been cited favorably or unfavorably by Shepardizing or KeyCiting it.

---

8. Some student-written law review pieces may become highly persuasive and lead to new legal theories being adopted by courts or legislatures. For example, the analysis and advocacy of a student law review article was relied on heavily by the California Supreme Court in the ground-breaking case *Sindell v. Abbott Laboratories*, 607 P.2d 924 (Cal. 1980), the first case to adopt market-share liability.

Table 8-3. Law Reviews and Journals Published by Tennessee Law Schools

Tennessee Journal of Law and Policy — University of Tennessee College of Law

Tennessee Journal of Practice and Procedure — University of Memphis School of Law

Tennessee Law Review — University of Tennessee College of Law

Transactions: The Tennessee Journal of Business Law — University of Tennessee College of Law

University of Memphis Law Review — University of Memphis School of Law

Vanderbilt Journal of Entertainment and Technology Law — Vanderbilt University Law School

Vanderbilt Journal of Transnational Law — Vanderbilt University Law School

Vanderbilt Law Review — Vanderbilt University Law School

B. Bar Journals

Each state's bar journal contains articles of particular interest to attorneys practicing in that state. The *Tennessee Bar Journal*, published monthly, is available in print and from Westlaw and LexisNexis. To access the *Tennessee Bar Journal* on Westlaw, use the database identifier TNBJ. Coverage is selective and starts in 1983. On LexisNexis, under the "Tennessee" tab, click "Law Review & Journals," then "Tennessee Bar Journal." Selective coverage begins in 2002. Many other state bar journals are also available online as well as on microfiche as part of *Hein's Bar Journal Microfiche Service*. The American Bar Association publishes the *ABA Journal*, which has articles of general interest to attorneys across the nation. The ABA also publishes related journals devoted to specific practice areas and interest groups, such as the *ABA Family Law Quarterly* and the *GP Solo & Small Firm Lawyer*.

Articles in bar journals are often shorter than the articles published in law reviews and do not have the extensive footnotes found in law review articles. Moreover, the bar journal articles have a practitioner's focus rather than the theoretical approach often found in academic law reviews and journals. Bar journals frequently include articles on topics such as law firm management, trends in law office technology, and step-by-step guides to complying with new court rules, as well as articles analyzing recent court decisions and newly enacted statutes.

C. Locating Articles

1. Westlaw and LexisNexis

Westlaw and LexisNexis both offer databases containing the full text of law review and journal articles. You may search either a database that combines the texts of many different law reviews, or a database with just one law review in it. To find these databases on Westlaw, go to the "Law Reviews, Bar Journals, and Legal Periodicals" menu of the Westlaw directory, or search the Westlaw directory database (database identifier IDEN) for the title you are looking for (for example, the *Harvard Law Review*). The most-frequently used Westlaw database containing multiple law reviews from all over the country is the JLR database. On LexisNexis, from the main "Legal" search page, look under the "Secondary Legal" menu for the link to "Law Reviews and Journals."

Another way to access law review articles on Westlaw and Lexis-Nexis is to use the services' topic menus. On LexisNexis, at the main "Legal" tab, click on "Area of Law – by Topic" to bring up a complete list of searchable topic collections. Clicking on "Environment," for example, brings up a list of databases with environmental law coverage, including a database that compiles articles from several leading environmental law journals. On Westlaw, go to the Westlaw Directory and click on "Topical Practice Areas" to display list of available topical collections. Click on "Environmental Law," then "Law Reviews, Legal Texts & Periodicals" to see the different databases of environmental law periodicals available.

Searching these online databases can be a fast and relatively easy way to locate recent, relevant law review articles. The authorities cited within the articles are typically hyperlinked, so that reading a case opinion you found cited in a law review article on LexisNexis or Westlaw is just a click away. Another advantage of using Westlaw or LexisNexis to read articles online is that you can efficiently use an online citator to see how later articles and even judicial opinions have treated the article you are reading.

There are, however, drawbacks to reading articles on Westlaw and LexisNexis. Always keep in mind that LexisNexis and Westlaw, for most of their law review databases, only provide articles written since the early 1990's or late 1980's. If you are interested in what earlier commentators had to say, Westlaw and LexisNexis will not be of use to you. Also, the formatting and display of the articles and their footnotes on LexisNexis and Westlaw will look very different from what you see in a book, and many people find them difficult to read and navigate in these formats.

2. Index to Legal Periodicals *and* LegalTrac

LexisNexis and Westlaw are not the only options for electronic access to law review articles. Many law libraries subscribe to separate web-based indexes that contain the full text of law review articles. The *Index to Legal Periodicals* includes citations to articles from over 1,000 journals in searchable format, as well as selected full-text articles. The coverage of *Index to Legal Periodicals* varies depending on the journal, but typically goes back to articles from 1981. An associated subscription that your library may offer, *Index to Legal Periodicals—Retro*, offers searchable access to citations from earlier law review articles (1918–1981). *LegalTrac* is another searchable database of citations. *LegalTrac* indexes over 1,200 law review titles and includes full text of the articles for about 125 of those titles.

While both *Index to Legal Periodicals* and *LegalTrac* include some full-text articles, their coverage has two drawbacks in common with the full-text coverage available on LexisNexis and Westlaw. First, the articles do not appear as they do in the actual law review books. The online articles can be difficult to read, and the technology used to transmit the text into these databases can cause occasional errors so that what the content of the database is not precisely correct. Since precision and clarity are very important in reading and citing to legal sources, it will often be necessary to locate the full text of an article in the hard copy volume or in a database that includes scanned images of the articles taken directly from the hard copy volumes. The second drawback to the coverage provided by *Index to Legal Periodicals* and *LegalTrac* is that their full-text coverage starts in the very recent past, so older articles are not available at all.

3. HeinOnline

HeinOnline is a database that helps overcome the drawbacks of researching law review articles on Westlaw, LexisNexis, *Index to Legal Periodicals*, and *LegalTrac*. *HeinOnline*[9] has full-text images of law review articles scanned directly from the law review books and presented as .pdf files. Coverage on *HeinOnline* varies, but typically starts with the prior year and goes as far back as a given law review or journal has been published.

There are three ways to retrieve law review articles on *HeinOnline*. First, on the main *HeinOnline* page,[10] you may choose to search the entire Law Journal Library, or various portions of it. Selecting the search function brings up a new page, allowing you to search either by author and title, or, using key words, to search the full text of all of the articles in the database. Searching in this large full-text database of law review articles can generate so many results that it is extremely difficult to find the best articles and those that are most relevant. It can also be tedious to wait for the website to conduct the search and present the results. While searching by author and title is more pre-

---

9. *HeinOnline* is actually a set of many databases. The Law Journal Library, the database discussed in this chapter, is only one of many. Other components of *HeinOnline* include full-text images of the entire *Federal Register*, the *United States Statutes at Large*, ALI proceedings, United Nations treaties, and many other valuable databases. However, the Law Journal Library is the most widely known and commonly used portion of this subscription series.

10. The exact address of the page and how to access it will vary depending on the institution's subscription and linking, so directions on how to get to the main *HeinOnline* page are not included here.

cise and quicker than searching the full text, neither search function is very efficient in yielding a manageable list of highly relevant results.

The second method for retrieving an article on *HeinOnline* is to use the "Quick Link" feature of *HeinOnline* to select the law review title you want and typing in the volume number and starting page number. The third method for retrieving an article on *HeinOnline* is to start by using *Index to Legal Periodicals* or *LegalTrac*, find a list of relevant articles, and then link directly from your search results in the index to the article on *HeinOnline*. Whether this type of direct linking is available will depend on the technology and services used by your law library. In general, look for a button or link in your *Index to Legal Periodicals* or *LegalTrac* search results that says something like "Full Text" or "Find Text."

4. Print Indexes

Your library may also offer print indexes to legal periodicals. The two most common are the *Current Law Index* and the *Index to Legal Periodicals and Books*. These titles allow searching either by subject or author. Using these volumes can be cumbersome and time-consuming, as you may have to consult several volumes if you are researching a span of years. However, some people find that using print indexes can lead them to better results since they can browse all entries in a subject heading rather than relying on the computer to produce results that are exact matches to search terms.

IV. *American Law Reports*

American Law Reports (A.L.R.) is a hybrid resource, offering both commentary on certain legal subjects and the full text of a few selected case opinions on those subjects. The commentary articles are called *annotations*. They tend to focus on very narrow topics, take a practitioner's view, and provide a survey of the law in different jurisdictions. An annotation on the exact topic of your research is likely to be extremely helpful. Annotations are written by lawyers who are knowledgeable, but not necessarily recognized experts.

Each annotation is accompanied by the full text of a leading case opinion on the topic. This case may contain different editorial enhancements from those in a reporter, but the court's opinion will be exactly the same.

> EXAMPLE: There is a conflict between some jurisdictions about the proper measure of damages due to the owner of a dog if the dog is killed or injured. A.L.R. reports a leading case on this issue, *Nichols v. Sukaro Kennels*, at 61 A.L.R. 5th 883 (Iowa 1996). The official cite for that case is 555 N.W.2d 689. In the same A.L.R. volume as the *Nichols* case is an annotation,[11] *Damages for Killing or Injuring Dog*, written by a lawyer, Robin Cheryl Miller. Among some of the topics discussed in this annotation are when damages are available for the owner's mental distress, when punitive damages are available, and what type of evidence will be admitted to establish the value of the dog.

Each annotation includes a detailed table of contents in outline format, references to related secondary authorities, a topical index, and a jurisdictional table of cited authorities. Because the annotations tend to be long, these tools can assist you in locating the portions of the work that address the specific subissue you are interested in or that are from your particular state.

There are several A.L.R. series. The early series contained both state and federal subjects. Currently, federal subjects are included in the series *A.L.R. Federal* while state subjects are included in numbered series: A.L.R. 3d through A.L.R. 6th. To locate an A.L.R. series in your library, search the library catalog for the title *American Law Reports*. You can also find these series as searchable databases on Westlaw and

---

11. The location in the A.L.R. volume of the full text of the opinion in relation to the corresponding annotation will vary depending on when the volume was published. You may find the case opinion immediately followed by the annotation or vice-versa. Recently A.L.R. has been published with all of the annotations at the front of the volume and case decisions grouped together at the back of each volume.

LexisNexis. The online versions will also usually include hyperlinks to related annotations and other secondary materials, as well as hyperlinks to the authorities cited within the annotation.

A.L.R. has several tools for finding helpful material. The *A.L.R. Index* is a multi-volume set that contains references to all of the numbered A.L.R. series as well as to the A.L.R. Fed. series. The *A.L.R. Digest* is organized in a similar fashion to case digests, with broad topics arranged alphabetically and their subtopics arranged in an outline format. In addition, the one-volume *A.L.R. Fed Quick Index* is available for finding annotations just in the A.L.R. Fed series, and a similar one-volume quick index is available for the third through sixth A.L.R. series.

The print versions of A.L.R. annotations are updated with pocket parts. You should also check the Annotation History Table in the index volumes to see whether an annotation has been supplemented or superseded by another annotation, rather than just updated with pocket parts. In the online versions of A.L.R. annotations, new cases and commentary are added directly into the text of the annotation, and superseding or supplementing annotations are accessible via hyperlink.

V. Topical Looseleaf Services

Looseleaf services are multi-volume sets of notebook-style publications devoted to a particular area of law. Frequently, they contain both primary and secondary sources, so that a practitioner or researcher in that area of law will have everything she needs at her fingertips. In topics such as tax and environmental law, a looseleaf service may contain statutes, administrative regulations, legislative history materials, summaries or the full text of judicial opinions and administrative decisions, commentary, information on pending legislation and cases, forms, checklists, and sample documents.

Looseleaf publications are called that because of the looseleaf, three-ring binders they have traditionally been published in. Updates are delivered to subscribers frequently. New pages can be inserted into the binders and old pages discarded, eliminating the need for researchers to check for pocket parts or separate supplements, or to wait until the end of the year for the most recent changes in the law to be noted. These looseleaf services can fill numerous volumes. The volumes may be arranged by topic, by state, or by another system.

A. Using Looseleaf Services in Print

Looseleaf services almost always have a "How to Use" section, generally near the beginning of the first volume. You should review this section before starting your research. You may also want to skim through a few volumes to become familiar with the organization of that particular service. Pay careful attention to each service's method and frequency of updating.

How you use a looseleaf service depends on what you know at the beginning of your research. In tax research, for example, if you need to look up a particular section of the Internal Revenue Code, go to the *Standard Federal Tax Reporter* and find the volume whose spine indicates that your code section is included. Turning to that section, you would find the statutory language, followed by related regulations issued by the Treasury Department. Next, you would see summaries of and citations to judicial decisions about the statute and administrative rulings of the Internal Revenue Service. At the end of the materials about your section of the Internal Revenue Code, you would find commentary written by the publisher.

If you do not know the particular section of the looseleaf that you need to research, begin with the topical index. Often this is the last volume of the series. Look up your research terms and write down the reference numbers given. These reference numbers will likely be paragraph or section numbers rather than page numbers. To maintain proper indexing despite frequent updates, looseleaf services are usually organized and indexed by paragraphs or sections. Even though the page numbers will change with future updates, the paragraph and section references will remain constant.

Turn to each paragraph or section number referenced in the index under your key terms. Browse the pages before and after your referenced paragraphs or sections, and check any tables of contents you might find at the beginning of a volume or chapter, to make sure that you have reviewed all relevant material.

B. Using Looseleaf Services Online

Many looseleaf services are available in electronic format. You may find them on CD-ROM, as searchable databases on LexisNexis or Westlaw, or via a paid subscription website. Electronic access will generally allow full-text searching, index browsing, or retrieving documents contained in the looseleaf by citation. For example, the *Standard Federal Tax Reporter* mentioned above is included as part of the *Tax Research Network* subscription website offered by Commerce Clearing House, the looseleaf's publisher.

Many of the subscription websites offer the user enhancements such as the options to save your research history, sign up for email updates and summaries of news in the area, participate in message boards and chat rooms with other legal professionals and researchers, learn from online tutorials, and receive live online help. If you are new to an online looseleaf service, make sure that you thoroughly explore your options and the available databases in order to get the most out of your research time.

To look for a version of a looseleaf service on LexisNexis, try searching the "Find a Source" feature with the name of the looseleaf you are looking for. On Westlaw, search the Westlaw directory (database identifier IDEN) with the name of the looseleaf you want to find.

VI. Restatements

A restatement is an organized and detailed summary of the common law in a specific legal area. Familiar titles include *Restatement of the Law of Contracts* and *Restatement of the Law of Torts*. Restatements are the results of collaborative efforts by committees of scholars, practitioners, and judges organized by the American Law Institute (ALI). These committees, led by a scholar called the *reporter*, draft text that explains the common law in rule format—with outline headings similar to statutes, rather than in the narrative format of judicial decisions. The committees circulate the drafts for review and revision. The restatement that is eventually published by the ALI includes the text of the rules that embody the common law together with commentary, illustrations, and notes from the reporter.

Restatements were originally intended simply to restate the law as it existed, in an effort to build national consistency in key common law areas. Over time, the authors of restatements grew more aggressive in drafting the restatements to reflect what the authors thought the law should be.

A portion of a restatement becomes primary authority only if it is adopted by a court in a particular case. After a court has adopted a portion of a restatement, the committee's commentary and illustrations, as well as any notes provided by the reporter, may be valuable tools in interpreting the restatement. Case opinions from other jurisdictions that have adopted the restatement will be persuasive authority.

To find a relevant restatement, search the library catalog using the key words "restatement" and "contracts" (or whatever other similar word might be in the title of the restatement you are looking for). Do not try exact title searches such as "Restatement of the Law of Contracts," which would result in missing relevant titles like "Restatement Second of the Law of Contracts." Also, keep in mind that many restatements are revised and rewritten over the years. You may be looking for a current restatement, or for an older restatement or draft of a restatement for historical research purposes. If you cannot find what you are looking for in print, try asking a law librarian if your law library subscribes to the microfiche set published by Hein, *American Law Institute's Archive Publications*, which includes all preliminary, proposed, tentative, and final drafts of the restatements produced by the ALI.

Many restatements and recent associated publications are available on Westlaw and LexisNexis as well. On Westlaw, the restatements, together with recent appendixes and pocket parts, are in the REST database. This database also includes current tentative drafts and discussion drafts of restatements. ALI's annual proceedings, which also include discussion and tentative drafts, can be found in the ALI-PRO-CEED database. On LexisNexis, click on the "Secondary Legal" heading, then look for the "Restatements" subheading to find current restatements, recent appendixes and supplements to the restatements, as well as current tentative and discussion drafts of restatements.

Restatements are typically only revised when a later version is published, although pocket parts and supplements are published frequently with citations to new case opinions that interpret the text of restatements. You may also use a citator service such as Shepard's or KeyCite to find cases and articles that cite the restatement section that you are researching.

VII. Uniform Laws and Model Codes

Uniform laws and model codes are written by organizations that hope to harmonize the statutory laws of the fifty states. The most active of these organizations is the National Conference of Commissioners on Uniform State Laws (NCCUSL). Much of the work of writing uniform laws and model codes is done by experts in the field who are law professors, judges, and practicing attorneys.

Familiar examples of these secondary sources include the *Uniform Commercial Code* (UCC) and the *Model Penal Code.* The typical way in which model and uniform codes are produced is that language is drafted, comments are solicited, and the language is revised and finalized. The published uniform law or model code includes both the proposed statutory language and explanatory notes from the authors.

Generally, you would research a uniform law or model code only after at least one of its provisions had been enacted in your jurisdiction. At the point a uniform law or model code is adopted by a legislature, that law or code becomes primary authority and its explanatory notes become very persuasive secondary authority. Reviewing the commentary could help you understand a statute in your jurisdiction that was based on the uniform or model language. For example, every state has adopted a version of the *Uniform Commercial Code.* Thus, you could gain insights into Tennessee's commercial code from commentary on the UCC on the provisions that were adopted by Tennessee. Additionally, judicial opinions from other states that adopted the same UCC provisions would be highly persuasive when interpreting Tennessee's statute.

Uniform laws and model codes, together with official notes and explanations, are published by their authors. Unofficial commercial versions add commentary and annotations summarizing judicial opinions that interpret the uniform laws and model codes. West publishes *Uniform Laws Annotated*, a multi-volume set of books that offers the text of those uniform laws prepared under the direction of NCCUSL, together with research annotations and extensive indexing and tables. The tables and other information in *Uniform Laws Annotated* provide a very quick and easy way to determine which states have adopted a particular uniform law or model code and, if one has been adopted, how it may have been amended or modified by that state. *Uniform Laws Annotated* is available as a searchable database on Westlaw (database identifier ULA). You may also find individual uniform laws and model codes, such as the *Model Penal Code* or the *Model Rules of Professional Conduct*, on either LexisNexis or Westlaw by searching the online services' directories for the title you are seeking.

VIII. Using Secondary Sources in Research

As the above discussions suggest, which source you use will depend on your research project. For a broad overview of an area of law, an encyclopedia may be best. For in-depth scholarly analysis on a narrower topic, a law review article is more likely to be helpful. On cutting-edge issues, CLE materials and bar journals may be helpful, as these sources often cover new areas of law promptly. In litigation, forms and pattern jury instructions may prove indispensable.

Despite the value of secondary sources, you will only occasionally cite them in memoranda and will rarely cite them in briefs. Encyclopedias, A.L.R. annotations, and CLE materials should be cited only as a last resort. Even sources that are considered highly persuasive secondary authority, such as a leading law review article or a well-respected treatise from your jurisdiction, should be cited infrequently, particularly in briefs.[12] Instead, cite to primary authority.

There are, however, three instances when citing secondary authorities is acceptable. First, sometimes you need to summarize the development of the law. If no case has provided that summary, citing a treatise or law review article that traces that development could be helpful to your reader. Second, citation to secondary authority is appropriate when there is no law on point for an argument you are making. For example, if you are tackling new legal issues, or arguing to change or expand the law, your only support might come from a law review article. Finally, secondary authority may provide additional support for a rule or argument for which you have also cited primary authority. For example, you can bolster an argument supported by a case opinion by also citing an article or treatise by a respected expert on the topic. This strategy maybe wise if the primary authority you are citing has come under attack.

Whether or not you cite a secondary source in a document, you must decide the weight to give secondary authority in developing your own analysis. Consider the following criteria:

- *Who is the author?* The views of a respected scholar, an acknowledged expert, or a judge carry more weight than a student author or anonymous editor.
- *When was the material published?* Especially for cutting-edge issues, a more recent article is more likely to be helpful. Even with more traditional issues, be sure that the material analyzes the current state of the law.
- *Where was the material published?* Articles published in established law journals are generally granted the most respect. A school's prestige and the length of the journal's existence influence how well established a journal is. A publication specific to your jurisdiction or dedicated to a particular topic,

---

12. It is more acceptable to cite secondary authorities (in addition to, rather than in lieu of, primary authorities) in intra-office legal memoranda. Doing so may prove helpful to another attorney or law clerk in your office who would like to do further research on the same topic.

however, may be more helpful than a publication from another state or one with a general focus.

- *What depth is provided?* The more focused and thorough the analysis, the more useful the material will be.
- *How relevant is it to your argument?* If the author is arguing your exact point, the material will be more persuasive than if the author's arguments are only tangential to yours.
- *Has this secondary source been cited previously by courts?* A court that has found an article or treatise persuasive in the past is more likely to find it persuasive again. You can use an online citator to see whether and how law review articles have been cited by courts. For treatises, try running a search juxtaposing the last name of the author and one of the words in the title in a case opinion database—preferably a database of just case law from your jurisdiction.

Chapter 9

Online Legal Research

I. Integrating Print and Online Research

Developing a comprehensive research strategy includes deciding when and how best to use online resources. Online resources include commercial providers like LexisNexis and Westlaw. Their databases contain enormous numbers of documents and their complex search engines enable the researcher to craft detailed requests. Free online resources maintained by government entities, universities, and law schools provide an increasing number of legal documents. Some of these sites have their own search engines. General search engines like Google and sites with non-legal information may be helpful resources as well.

This chapter reviews some questions you should ask to determine whether to use online sources instead of print sources, outlines some available online resources, and explains how to conduct research online. Appendix A, at the end of the book, includes references to websites for finding Tennessee law online.

II. Choosing Print or Online Sources

Online research has a number of advantages. Most significant among those are ease of searching, the ability to navigate among hyperlinked documents, the convenience of downloading or printing important documents, and the frequency with which many online sources are updated. Nevertheless, online searching is not always the most effective or cost-efficient way to conduct your research. Most experienced legal researchers agree that *beginning* research with books, then moving to online sources, is generally more productive than beginning online. Ask yourself the following questions in deciding whether to use online sources instead of books.

A. How much do you know about the topic?

When a field of law or particular issue is new to you, you will likely have difficulty coming up with the right search terms to generate relevant results with online searching. You may not know the terms of art used by lawyers, legislators, or judges when discussing your issue, or you may not realize that a particular defense, cause of action, or theory is likely to figure prominently into case opinions about your topic. If this is a new field of law or issue for you, it is probably safest and most efficient to start in a print secondary source where you can scan a table of contents and browse through relevant portions of the book. Once you feel comfortable with an area of law, you can move on to do efficient online searching.

B. Are your search terms likely to be broad or narrow?

List your likely search terms. How general or specific are they? Are they likely to be used in many different contexts, only some of which would be relevant to your research? If so, it may be best to start researching in print. For example, if you were researching when police detention of a possible witness or suspect turned into arrest for purposes of *Miranda* rights, your search terms might include words such as police, detain, detention, arrest, interrogation, warning, and Miranda. All of these terms could be used in myriad legal situations and could very well appear in a tremendously high number of published opinions in criminal cases in the country—the vast majority of which would have nothing to do with what you are researching. Trying to find a way to tell the computer exactly what you want in this situation will be difficult. But by starting with a good book on search and seizure law and skimming through the table of contents, one could quickly and easily discover the important issues and leading authorities in that area of law.

If, on the other hand, you can quickly come up with specific search terms, then it may be more efficient to start research online. For example, if you are trying to find and summarize cases in which someone was injured because a car's air bag failed to deploy in an accident, you have some very good and specific search terms to work with, such as air bag, airbag, accident, crash, deploy, and inflate. Running online searches in case law databases would likely be a strong strategy.

C. How much does it cost, and who is paying?

Print sources are "free" in the sense that the library has already paid for them. The cost of purchasing and storing print sources continues to rise, and some libraries are finding that online services are less expensive. If you cannot find a source you need in the library, online searching may be your only alternative.

Online sources provided by governments and universities are usually free. When cost is an issue, consider using these sources first, but do not assume that all commercial sites for computer searches are too expensive. A quick Shepard's or KeyCite search online, with a printout of the results to be found in the stacks, will almost always be much more efficient than spending hours poring over Shepard's print volumes that are hard to read and not as up-to-date as what you would find on the computer.

Other methods of online searching with LexisNexis and Westlaw may be relatively inexpensive as well. Law firms are finding that they can negotiate reasonable flat rates that allow access to the narrow set of online sources that those firms use routinely in their practice. However, if your firm does not have a flat-rate access package with LexisNexis or Westlaw, the costs of searching can be tremendous. Factors that affect those costs include the number of minutes you are logged on, the number of searches you conduct, the size of the databases you search, and how many documents you choose to print. The typical charge for access to an online search service such as LexisNexis or Westlaw (other than on the flat-rate plans) is between three and five dollars per minute, exclusive of printing charges. A single research project, poorly conceived and sloppily done, could costs hundreds or thousands of dollars. Be sure you know the billing practices of your office before deciding to use online sources that are not free: What is your office's contract with the online provider? How will your office pass along charges to clients? How much are the clients willing to pay? Are there any databases that are considered off-limits to the attorneys, due to the expense? When you do pro bono work, will the firm cover the costs of online searches?

Even if your firm does have a flat-rate access package, keep in mind that extensive use of LexisNexis or Westlaw in the current year by people in your firm will often mean that the price of the package next year will be much higher. Therefore, it is always prudent to try to be as efficient as possible on LexisNexis or Westlaw, even if your firm subscribes to a flat rate, unlimited use access plan.

D. Which is more important: accuracy and official status of the documents, or currency of the documents?

Print material tends to be more accurate than online material. The very process of publishing ensures a high level of reliability. For a book to appear in a law library, the publisher must first have decided the material in the book had some value. The publisher and author would have edited the document numerous times. Next, a law librarian must have decided that the book would enhance the collection. The publisher, author, and librarian presumably have reputations to protect through making careful decisions. Because of this careful selection process, print material tends to be more accurate than online versions of the same documents.

In contrast to the time-intensive process of publishing print sources, online material is often made available very quickly, making it valuable to those who need to stay on top of changes in the law. This rapid availability means, though, that even reputable services post documents with less editing than a book would warrant. Trusted sources like Westlaw and LexisNexis tend to have more typographical errors in their online documents than in their print counterparts. Government websites are usually highly reliable, but even the online documents that governments post may not be considered "official." For example, the official version of a Tennessee judicial decision is found in *West's South Western Reporter;* the version posted by the Tennessee Supreme Court on its own website is unofficial.[1]

A large body of information is available online outside of the well-known services and trusted sites, and not all of it is good information. Some of this information may not have been subjected to any quality controls; for a document to appear on a website, a person simply has to know how to post it. Examples of extremely poor-quality legal "information" that may be found on the Internet include the myriad "dumb laws" sites, where many of the "dumb laws" appear to have been made up but are presented as fact, and various "tax protest" websites in which lay authors make unfounded, but authoritative-sounding, claims that the Constitution forbids the collection of income tax.

If a high level of accuracy is important, or if you must have the official version of documents you are researching, you will want to carefully investigate the authenticity of what is available online versus in print and keep that in mind when deciding which sources to use in your research. However, if it is crucial that your research be up-to-date, online sources will be your best bet. Even if accuracy and official status are your top criteria and you decide to use print sources, you will almost always need to use an online citator to update your research.

---

1. More and more, however, state governments are designating online versions of their authorities as official versions. For example, Tennessee's administrative code and register are both available only online, and the state's electronic version is considered official.

Table 9-1. Websites of Commercial Providers

Provider	Main Web Address	Law Student Web Address
Lexis-Nexis	www.lexisnexis.com	www.lexisnexis.com/lawschool
Loislaw	www.loislaw.com	www.loislawschool.com
VersusLaw	www.versuslaw.com	www.versuslaw.com/subscribe/vslStudentReg.asp
Westlaw	www.westlaw.com	www.lawschool.westlaw.com

III. Online Sources for Legal Research

A legal researcher can increase the chances of finding accurate material by using highly regarded and dependable sites. The following are examples of established, reputable online research sites. For each site, look for a link such as "Help" or "Search Tips" to provide information about how best to find material on that site. Some sites also offer online tutorials to introduce their resources and search processes.

A. Commercial Providers

LexisNexis and Westlaw are the largest commercial providers of computerized legal research. Both have reputations for accurate material and powerful search techniques. They provide extensive, nationwide coverage of primary and secondary authorities. Other commercial providers of legal materials include Loislaw and VersusLaw. They tend to be much less expensive than Westlaw and LexisNexis, but they also provide less extensive coverage and less powerful searching. Some of these providers allow you a free trial to search their sites before deciding whether to subscribe to their services. Many online commercial legal research vendors also offer special portals or sites specifically tailored to law students, and a school's subscription may require beginning from one of these special law student pages. Table 9-1 provides the web addresses for some of the major commercial vendors of online legal research materials.

B. Government Websites

Government entities often provide access to information on their websites for free. These sites contain less information than is available from the commercial providers, and the search engines on these sites tend to be less powerful. However, the information available on government websites is increasing, making them more useful research tools.

Tennessee, like many other states, maintains websites for some of its primary authority. The official versions of the *Official Compilation of the Rules and Regulations of the State of Tennessee* and the *Tennessee Administrative Register* are the free, online versions published by the Tennessee Secretary of State. The official versions of the Tennessee session laws are also published online by the state legislature. In addition, Tennessee provides unofficial electronic versions of recent appellate court opinions.[2] A chart in Appendix A to this book contains useful websites for Tennessee research. The primary limitation to the free sites is that their material may be available only for recent years.

IV. How to Make the Most of Online Searching

A. General Considerations in Searching Online

Many novice legal researchers tend to work too quickly, without stopping to consider exactly what document they are looking at, what value it has, or what their options are for changing either the materials they are researching or their search techniques. The following

---

2. Unlike many other states, Tennessee's state government does not offer a free, online version of the Tennessee statutory code. However, the code's official publisher, LexisNexis, does provide free online access to an unofficial, unannotated version of the code, found at www.michie.com.

factors should be weighed throughout the online legal research process in order to make sure that your results are accurate and current and that your search methods are efficient and focused.

1. What type of authority is your document?

In print sources, cases, statutes, and commentary usually appear in different books. When looking in a reporter, you know that you are reading a case opinion, not a statute or a law review article. Cases, statutes, and commentary look very different from one another in print sources. In contrast, many documents appear the same on a computer screen; for example, a federal statute on a government site and a law student's paraphrased outline of that statute on his personal web page may be shown online in the same font with the same layout.

The difficulty in distinguishing between online documents is compounded because hyperlinks in online sources allow you to jump from a case to a statute to an article in a few clicks of the mouse. In an actual library, those moves may take you to different shelves or different floors. While it is convenient to stay in front of a computer, when reading a document online, you need to pay careful attention to what the document actually is because you can easily lose track of the many different types of sources you click into. As you become a more experienced researcher, you will more quickly be able to distinguish documents online, and the benefits of using print material may decrease.

2. Who offers the website? What kind of quality does it have?

As noted earlier in this chapter, anyone who has access to the Internet and knows a little bit about computers can post just about anything on the web. Be extremely leery of documents that you find hosted on websites such as geocities.com or angelfire.com that allow anyone to post anything on a personal website. Look at the domain name of the website: government sites ending in *.gov, *.mil, or *.us; educational sites ending in *.edu; or non-profit organization sites ending in *.org are generally considered to provide higher-quality information than what you can find posted on someone's personal website.

High-quality sites with good information presented will tell you when they were last updated. Depending on the type of materials presented, that will generally be quite recently. Good, useful sites will include links to help navigate or search the site. They will also provide contact information for the person or organization responsible for the site, and that contact information will be more than just an email address.

You may also wish to check to see whether the site you are looking at is well thought of by others. You can assess whether a site is highly trafficked, read subjective reviews, and find out what other sites have linked to the site you are assessing. Go to www.alexa.com, click on "Traffic Rankings," and then enter the URL of the website you are researching. You can also go to www.google.com and type in *link*: followed immediately (no space) by the URL of the site you are researching. This search will generate a list of sites that link to the site you are researching. If your site is linked to by many other reputable organizations' websites, that would be a reliable indicator of high quality.

3. When was the document published?

As noted above, currency is very important. In book research, the copyright date shows when a book's contents were published. In secondary sources, digests, annotated statutes, and other resources, updates are often included in pocket parts or freestanding supplements shelved nearby. While it is easy to determine the date of publication and updating of print sources, these sources are rarely as up-to-date as online sources. But just because you are searching online, you cannot assume that the specific document you are looking at, or the database you are using, is the most current and up-to-date resource available. Thus, you should look for a date on the online document stating when it was published or posted.

You should also question the period of time that an online data-base covers. Be sure to check every online site or database you use for its scope of coverage, if that information is available. For instance, some online sites may contain materials from only the last few years. If you are researching tort law, and the leading *res ipsa loquitur* case from your jurisdiction was published thirty years ago, you might have a very hard time locating it online using only free government web-sites. Finding older material may require using print sources in some instances.

4. How can online tools and context be used to improve searching?

An increasing number of online sources include tables of con-tents, hyperlinked outlines, browseable page formats, and indexes. These tools can provide context so that a researcher can understand the big picture before concentrating on a narrow legal issue. They can also help you make sure that you have found all relevant ma-terials, rather than just the few portions of an online text that ex-actly correspond to the precise words you used in your search query.

When searching online, use these tools whenever they are avail-able. Clicking on a table of contents link can show you where your document is placed within related material. This tactic is especially helpful when an online search lands you in the middle of a large doc-ument and you lack the visual clues or context to understand how that document relates to the bigger picture.

Many lawyers—from novices to experts—have stories about the great case or article that they stumbled across in the library stacks while looking for something else. These stories result not just from serendipity, but from being near the area in a resource that puts re-lated information together. Sometimes online searching also produces a serendipitous result; if you feel you may be close but are not find-ing the exact material you need, try using an online table of contents, outline, or index link to reorient yourself.

B. Nuts and Bolts of Searching Westlaw and LexisNexis

Each website has a different method for retrieving information, though all tend to follow the same algorithms. Because most websites are constantly being revised and because their search methods change over time, this overview provides only general information that is likely to be useful in the long run. The following explanations focus on LexisNexis and Westlaw, though much of the information should be transferable to other online sources.[3]

1. Retrieving a Document When You Have a Citation

When you have a citation to a case opinion, statute, article, or other legal source, retrieving that document online is as simple, and as complicated, as typing the citation into a designated box on the proper screen. In LexisNexis, click on the "Get a Document" tab and type in the citation. If you do not know the citation, but know the name of the case you are looking for, after clicking on "Get a Document," click on the "Party Name" tab and fill in as much as you know with respect to party names, jurisdiction, and date of decision. In Westlaw, use the box on the left of the screen labeled "Find by citation." Enter your citation and click the "Go" button. If you do not know the citation but know of the name of the case you are looking for, click the "Find &

---

3. In addition, LexisNexis and Westlaw provide ample training material in print and on their websites. For research assistance, call LexisNexis at 1-800-455-3947 and Westlaw at 1-800-733-2889. Both services also offer an instant messaging help feature which you can access by following the "Help" (on Westlaw) or "Live Support" (on LexisNexis) links on your screen. While in law school, if your research instructor permits use of these resources, you should take advantage of them. Your law school library is paying for this assistance for you as part of the subscription package; there is no sense in floundering around aimlessly when research experts are standing by waiting to help you for free. Also, many law firms provide free in-house training for LexisNexis and Westlaw. Again, take advantage of training opportunities when they arise.

Print" link toward the top of the screen, then click the "Find a Case by Party Name" link on the left side of the resulting screen.

How can this be complicated? LexisNexis and Westlaw have thousands of different publications in their databases. In order for the system to recognize your citation and retrieve the correct document, you must use the right database abbreviation. This isn't usually challenging if you are working with a citation to a common case reporter, such as S.W.2d or F.2d. However, if you are looking for a law review article, or a statute from a jurisdiction you don't do much work in, you will need to be careful to use the correct abbreviation. To find the right abbreviation on Westlaw, after clicking the "Find & Print" link, click on the "Publications List" link on the left-hand side of the resulting screen. This will bring up a list of Westlaw publications with associated abbreviations, which you can search or browse. On Lexis-Nexis, after clicking on "Get a Document," look for the "Citation Formats" link. Again, you can search or browse the resulting list.[4]

2. Continuing Research with "One Good Case"

Once you find an authority that is on point, you can use it as a springboard to find other relevant sources. In Westlaw, once you pull up a case using the "Find" function or by searching, the left frame of the page displaying the case will include a "Results Plus" column. Results Plus is an automatically generated list of secondary sources that have cited your case or that contain many of the same key words. You can explore the secondary sources from Results Plus to see if they cite more authorities on your topic. Keep in mind that in law practice, linking to Results Plus documents may result in additional charges to your firm. You may also look in the left-hand frame under the "KeyCite" heading for the "Citing References" link. Clicking Citing References will retrieve a list of additional case opinions and secondary authorities that have cited your case. When you have retrieved the citing references, look for the "Limit KeyCite Display" button (usually at the bottom of the page).

---

4. Abbreviation formats to use with "Find" and "Get a Document" for some of the more common Tennessee materials are included in Appendix A to this book.

This link will allow you to narrow your citing references to display only the case opinions that address the issues you are most interested in.

Another way to use Westlaw to find additional authorities when you have one relevant case opinion is to use the West topic and key number system. After finding a case on point, identify the topics and key numbers for the relevant headnotes. Then use these headnotes to search the online version of the West digest system for more cases that address the same points of law. Clicking on a key number in the headnotes at the beginning of the case will bring up a screen that prompts a search for additional cases with that topic and key number. Note that in online searching the topic is reduced to a number that precedes a "k" and the key number follows. For example, the topic "Environmental Law" is assigned the online number 149E. Thus, the topic-key number "Environmental Law 528" on endangered species is presented online as 149Ek528. Outline headings next to online topics and key numbers tell you what they mean. You are not expected to somehow know that 149Ek528 means endangered species.

You also have several options on LexisNexis to proceed with your research once you have one good case. One step that you can take is to click on the "Shepardize" button to see other case opinions and secondary authorities that cite your case. By restricting your Shepard's search to relevant headnotes, you can narrow the displayed results to those subsequent cases that are most likely to address the issues you are particularly interested in. Other LexisNexis options include the "More Like This" or "More Like Selected Text" functions, which ask the computer to find other case opinions with similar citations or similar language.

3. Researching a Legal Issue from Scratch

Often your work will require you to begin your research with no leads and no cites to authorities relevant to your issue. This section explains the process you should use in these situations. If you are new to online legal searches, your searches may be more successful if you complete the chart in Table 9-2 before beginning a search. Even after you become experienced in online searching, you should still keep

Table 9-2. Example Notes for Online Searching

Date of Search: *June 19, 2007*

Issue: *Whether a covenant not to compete is enforceable in Tennessee*

Online Service: *Westlaw*

Database(s) Searched: *Tennessee cases (database identifier: TN-CS)*

Search Terms: *Covenant, contract, competition, noncompetition, restraint of trade, compete, non-compete, employer, employee, employment*

Date Restriction: *Last three years*

Search: *(Covenant contract) /p (noncompet! "restraint of trade" compet!) /p employ!*

Results: *[Either list your results here or print a cite list to attach to your notes.]*

---

notes containing the dates you searched, the searches you ran, and your results from the searches. These notes will help you stay on track while avoiding duplicating your research at a later date. Notes will also indicate the time period that needs to be updated as you near your project deadline.[5] Example notes are in Table 9-2.

a. Choose a Database

First determine whether you will use LexisNexis or Westlaw. Sometimes you will have access to just one service, for example, if your office subscribes only to Westlaw. If you do have a choice, consider your familiarity with each service,[6] the power and efficiency of the search

---

5. Although LexisNexis and Westlaw both save your prior searches and research information ("Research Trail" on Westlaw and "History" on LexisNexis), this information is kept only for a relatively brief period of time.

6. If you are in law school working on an academic project, you should strongly consider using the service with which you are less comfortable on a regular basis. You will be expected to be proficient in both LexisNexis and Westlaw when applying for and working in legal jobs, and the best way to become proficient is to practice using these systems to develop your skills.

options afforded to you, the breadth of resources available through the service, and the cost of the service.

After deciding whether to use LexisNexis or Westlaw, you must then choose which database or databases to search. LexisNexis and Westlaw divide their vast resources into groups by type of document, topic, and jurisdiction. In LexisNexis, these databases are called "sources." In Westlaw, they are referred to simply as databases. Each service has a directory that allows you to identify the databases in which you wish to search. You may also use the "Find a Source" search function on LexisNexis, or search the Westlaw directory (database identifier IDEN), to find databases. Until you are extremely comfortable with LexisNexis and Westlaw, you should always explore your options before deciding which database to search. Although LexisNexis and Westlaw offer quick links to a few selected databases on their opening pages, you should not fall into the trap of thinking that those quick links are your only, or your best, options. LexisNexis and Westlaw both tend to use quick links to promote some of their largest, most generic, and most expensive databases.

Try to restrict your search to the smallest database or set of databases that will contain the documents you need. Because online databases correspond to many of the books you have used, it may be helpful to think of yourself in the stacks of the library when choosing databases. Do you really want to search the contents of every reporter in the library, or do you want to search just Tennessee case opinions? In addition to producing a more focused set of results, smaller databases also tend to be less expensive than their larger counterparts.

b. Generate Search Terms

Just as in print research, you must generate a list of search terms for online research. Review Chapter 1 for suggestions on generating a comprehensive list of terms.

How you use the terms in online searching is different from how you use them in print research. In print, you look for the terms in indexes and tables of contents to find relevant portions of books. Sometimes this is referred to as "conceptual research" because you are searching indexes for concepts that lawyers have used over time to describe a cause of action, defense, or remedy.

In contrast, in online searching you will most often use these words to search the full text of documents. This is called "full text" searching. There can be disadvantages with this search method. If the author of a particular document does not use the exact term you are searching for, you will not find that document in your results.

c. Construct a Search

Typing in a string of key words the way you might do at a typical web search engine is likely to result in frustration and muddied results. Searching on LexisNexis and Westlaw is more powerful, and thus requires more thought and more skill on your part. Although you are using a search box that likely looks very similar to other search boxes you have used in general search engines before, searching LexisNexis or Westlaw is very different from searching the Internet with Google or Yahoo.

i. Using Boolean Connectors

More comprehensive searches usually result from the use of Boolean[7] connectors. These connectors tell the computer how the terms should be placed in relation to one another in targeted documents, enabling you to more accurately control what the computer searches for. To use Boolean connectors effectively, think of the ideal document you would like to find and try to imagine where your search terms would be located in relationship to each other within that document. Would they be in the same sentence? The same paragraph? Table 9-3 summarizes the most common connectors and commands. Although LexisNexis and Westlaw share many of the same

---

7. George Boole was a British mathematician. The Boolean connectors that carry his name dictate the logical relationship of search terms to each other.

Boolean connectors and default search assumptions, there are significant differences between the two services as well.

Using the example notes in Table 9-2, searching the terms *(covenant contract) /p (noncompet! "restraint of trade" compet!) /p employ!* on Westlaw, the computer will look for:

* either the term *covenant* or *contract*
* within the same paragraph as the terms *noncompetitive* or *competitive*, or varations such as *noncompetition* or *competitor*; or within the same paragraph as the phrase *restraint of trade*
* and also in that paragraph variations of *employ, employee, employer, employment.*

Misuse of Boolean connectors, or getting confused about which connectors to use on LexisNexis or Westlaw, can produce bizarre search results. If, on Westlaw, a researcher forgot to put quote marks around "restraint of trade," the results would include any case opinion in which the word *restraint* was used or in which the word *trade* was used. That is because Westlaw assumes that any two words in a search string that are not connected with quotation marks or a Boolean connector such as "/p" are alternative search terms rather than a phrase. So searching on Westlaw for *statute of frauds* without quotation marks will produce all the documents that refer to either a statute or to fraud, rather than just the documents that contain references to the *statute of frauds.* Conversely, on LexisNexis, the computer will make a default assumption that words next to each other are to be searched as a phrase, and only as a phrase. This default assumption has a tendency to trip up novice legal researchers who are more familiar with general-interest Internet search engines. If you are used to simply typing in a string of words that might have some relevance to what you are looking for, the fact that the computer will assume you mean those as an exact phrase, and nothing else, can come as a surprise. If you type in *covenant contract noncompetition* on LexisNexis, you will only retrieve documents that contain the precise phrase, "covenant contract noncompetition." Since that's a rather unlikely phrase, you'll probably retrieve no documents whatsoever.

Table 9-3. Boolean Connectors and Commands

Goal	Westlaw	LexisNexis
To find alternative terms anywhere in the document	*Leave blank space Example:* covenant contract	*Use or Example:* covenant or contract
To find both terms anywhere in the document	*Use and Example:* covenant and contract	*Use and Example:* covenant and contract
To find both terms within the same sentence	*Use /s Example:* contract /s competition	*Use /s Example:* contract /s competition
To find both terms within the same paragraph	*Use /p Example:* contract /p competition	*Use /p Example:* contract /p competition
To find both terms within a particular distance from each other	*Use /75 Example:* contract /75 competition *will result in documents with the term contract within 75 words of the term competition*	*Use /75 Example:* contract /75 competition *will result in documents with the term contract within 75 words of the term competition*
To find terms used as a phrase	*Put the phrase in quotation marks Example:* "covenant not to compete"	*No quotation marks necessary Example:* covenant not to compete
To exclude terms	*Use but not Example:* RICO but not "Puerto Rico"	*Use and not Example:* RICO and not Puerto Rico
To find variants of a term	*Add ! to end of word root Example:* employ! *will retrieve employ, employment, employer, employed, employee*	*Add ! to end of word root Example:* employ! *will retrieve employ, employment, employer, employed, employee*

ii. Natural Language Searching

LexisNexis and Westlaw allow natural language searching, which may be most similar to the online searching you have done in the past. Simply type in a question or a list of words and let the computer decide which words are critical, whether the words should appear in some proximity to one another, and how often they appear in the document.

Natural language searching is most useful when you are looking for one or two good authorities to start your research. Because of its imprecise nature, it will never retrieve an exhaustive list of relevant authorities, and thus should never be used as the sole method of research. However, it can be a useful starting place, especially when you are working with search terms that are rather general in nature and might appear, at least in passing, in many different documents. Performing a natural language search should bring up a short list of results[8] that contain your search terms very frequently. Thus, this type of search eliminates the problem of putting in good search terms, getting hundreds of results, and being faced with the daunting prospect of sifting through them to determine which are the best to use to start your research.

If you use a natural language search early in your research, you may find that one good case to spark more research. Natural language searching is also effective when searching large databases of secondary materials such as law review articles. Finding the one or two most relevant law review articles is much easier with natural language searching than with Boolean connectors. Skimming the law review article footnotes may then lead you to a particularly good case. Once you find your one good case, use its topics and key numbers (on Westlaw), or its core terms (on LexisNexis), or Shepardize or KeyCite it to find more case opinions.

iii. Topic Searching

Both LexisNexis and Westlaw allow searching by topic. On Lexis-Nexis, the service is called Search Advisor. With Search Advisor, you can search for a particular topic or browse through a hyperlinked outline of legal topics. The topics are broken into subtopics, and moving through the hyperlinked outline eventually brings up a screen where you can search for case opinions on that subtopic. Some

---

8. Both LexisNexis and Westlaw have a default number of limited results that will be retrieved using a natural language search. On LexisNexis, to change this default number, click the "Preferences" link in the upper right corner of the screen. To change the default number on Westlaw, click on the "Preferences" link in the upper right corner of the screen, the "Search" link on the left-hand frame of the resulting screen.

subtopics also have associated administrative agency materials or secondary authorities for you to search.

On Westlaw, the topic-searching service is called KeySearch. Again, you can either search for a particular topic or subtopic, or browse a menu of legal topics. Clicking through the menus of topics will allow you to search for case opinions and secondary sources addressing your particular issue. For example, if you were looking for law review articles and case opinions addressing the reintroduction of wolves in the American west, you would start by clicking on "Environmental Law." "Environmental Law" would then expand into a sub-menu with many different options, including air pollution, endangered and protected species, historic preservation, and nuclear power. By selecting endangered species, you get another sub-menu with several different fields of law. One of those is "Wolves." Click on "Wolves," and you can search case opinions from different jurisdictions, encyclopedias, A.L.R. series, or law review articles on wolves. You can also enter additional search terms (for example, "Yellowstone") to make sure your search will be as targeted as possible.

iv. Segment and Field Searching

Both LexisNexis and Westlaw allow you to search specific parts of documents, such as the names of the parties involved, the author, or the court. To search for cases in which the Boeing Company was a named party, you need to be able to tell the computer to retrieve only those cases, rather than all case opinions in which Boeing was mentioned in passing, or in which the judge cited to another published case involving Boeing. To do that, look on LexisNexis for "Segments" drop down menus and on Westlaw for "Field" drop down menus. Choose the particular area of the document you wish to search, type in your search terms, and click to add the language to your search query. So, to find cases on Westlaw in which Boeing was a party, use the Field menu to select the "Title" field and type in "Boeing" as your field search term.

Many new legal researchers, simply because they are unfamiliar with these features, do not use them even though doing so could significantly narrow and improve their search results. Whenever you are using a new database on LexisNexis or Westlaw, explore the available segments or fields and consider whether they would prove useful in your searching.

v. Expanding or Restricting Your Search

Many of your initial searches will locate either no documents or more than 1,000 documents. Do not become frustrated. With practice, you will learn to craft more precise searches that produce more helpful results.

If a search produces no results, use broader connectors (e.g., search for terms in the same paragraph rather than in the same sentence), use more alternative terms, or use a larger database. If you still find nothing, consider reading a secondary source to increase your understanding of the issue, researching in print sources, or checking with your supervising attorney.

If your search produces a long list of results, skim them to see whether they are on point. If the results seem irrelevant, modify your search query by omitting broad terms, using more restrictive connectors, or using a smaller database. You may also wish to consider switching to a natural language search in order to find a few very pertinent results. Another tactic is to use the "Locate in Result" feature on Westlaw or the "Focus" feature on LexisNexis to narrow your results further. These features allow you to construct a search within your results, producing a subset of results that contain the new search terms you put in. These features are cost efficient because they do not result in the additional charges of a new search.

Chapter 10

Research Strategies and Organization

I. Moving from Story to Strategy

In practice, a client will come to your office with a problem and ask for help in solving it. A client without much legal experience will focus on facts that are important to him, without regard to whether they are legally significant. The client may have a desired solution in mind; that solution may best be obtained through legal remedies, or through mediation, family counseling, management strategies, or other means.

Your job will be to sift through the client's story to identify the legal issues. This may include asking questions to probe for facts the client may not immediately bring up but which have important legal consequences. Your job may also include reviewing documents such as contracts, letters, bills, or public records. In addition, you may need to interview other people who are involved in the client's situation.

Sometimes you will not be able to identify the legal issues immediately. Especially in an unfamiliar area of law, you may need to do some additional research to learn about the legal issues that affect the client's situation. Once you have some background in the relevant law, you should determine which legal issues affect the client's situation and begin to formulate a comprehensive research strategy.

II. Planning Your Research Strategy

A. The Research Process

The research process presented in Chapter 1 contains seven steps: (1) generate a list of *research terms*; (2) consult *secondary sources*; (3) find controlling *constitutional provisions, statutes, regulations*, or *rules*; (4) find citations to relevant *case law*; (5) read the full text of the cases; (6) *update* your primary authorities using a citator such as Shepard's or KeyCite; and (7) know you are finished when you *encounter the same authorities* and no new authorities through all the research methods you employ. After learning how to use each of the resources listed, you can modify this basic process and design a research strategy that is appropriate for a specific project.

When researching an unfamiliar area of law, you will probably be more successful if you begin with secondary sources. In contrast, if you are familiar with an area of statutory law from previous work, your research may be more effective if you go directly to an annotated code. As a third example, if you are working for another attorney who gives you a citation to a case she knows is relevant, you may want to begin by updating the case or using its topics and key numbers in a West digest. Finally, if your supervisor knows that the issue is controlled by common law, you may feel comfortable not researching statutory or constitutional provisions, or spending very little time in those areas.

The research process is not necessarily linear. Research terms are useful in searching the indexes of secondary sources and statutes as well as digests. Secondary sources may cite relevant statutes or cases. Updating may reveal more cases that you need to read, or it may uncover a new law review article that is on point. As you learn more about a project, you may want to review whether your earlier research was effective. Even as you begin writing, you may need to do more research if new issues arise or if you need more support for an argument.

B. Creating Your Research Plan

The first document you should create before you begin substantive research is your *research plan*. Particularly as a novice legal researcher, you will find that writing up your research plan will help you clarify issues and think about where to begin. A sample research plan can be seen in Table 10-1. Before you start your first legal job, you may want to devise a plan of your own and keep it available on your computer or in print. Having a form with questions already on it is much more organized and efficient than simply writing down lists of words or sources. If you were using the form in Table 10-1, you would keep the right-hand column blank on your master copy and fill in the blanks for each new research project you were assigned.

Imagine that you are just starting for first legal clerking job in a big firm in Nashville. You are called into the assigning attorney's office and told the following:

> Our client is Private Detection, Inc. P.D.I. contracts with various government agencies to build, staff, and run jails, prisons, and juvenile detention facilities. One of its facilities is a local juvenile detention facility, the "Abigail Samuels Home for Wayward Youth." Recently, a female employee at the Abigail Samuels Home requested a transfer from being a group leader in the girls' wing to being a group leader in the boys' wing. The human services department of P.D.I. has tentatively denied the request but has asked us to make sure the department is complying with all laws. The head of human services denied the request because she is concerned about privacy considerations for the young male juveniles. The position of group leader requires the employee to conduct full body searches and supervise bathroom areas. Research whether this situation would qualify for an exception to the prohibition against sex discrimination in employment. Start by looking at Title VII and other federal law. Please give me a memorandum on this issue next Monday.

Having a worksheet that you regularly use will make a new project seem less overwhelming, since the plan will set out boundaries for

Table 10-1. Sample Research Plan

Issue Statement	*Is it sex-based employment discrimination to refuse to transfer a female employee to work with boys in a juvenile detention facility when privacy concerns are involved?*
Jurisdiction	*Start with federal, preferably 6th Circuit*
Known relevant authorities	*Title VII*
Terms of art or legal jargon to define before beginning research	*None*
Research terms	*Sex-based, gender, male, female, man, woman, employment discrimination, employ!, Title VII, jail, prison, juvenile detention, inmate, prisoner, bathroom, privacy*
Possible secondary sources	*Nutshell or hornbook on employment discrimination, A.L.R. Federal*
Possible statutes	*United States Code Annotated*
Possible regulations	*Code of Federal Regulations*
Case law databases or reporters	*CTA6, DCT6, ALLFEDS (Westlaw)*
Period of time to research	*Current*
Follow-up questions for supervising attorney	*Should I look at state law at all or just research federal law?*
Due date and desired format of work product	*Office memorandum due Monday, July 3*

your research and suggest the steps you need to take for each project. Furthermore, if you form the habit of working with your form and taking it with you to meetings with assigning attorneys, you will have a better chance of getting all the information you need to begin researching right away. This means you won't have to repeatedly go back to your assigning attorney to clarify issues such as jurisdiction or due date that the attorney neglected to mention and you forgot to ask about in your meeting.

You should refer to this document frequently to be sure you are keeping on track. Once you write out your research plan, you can think about where in your research process online sources will be more efficient than print sources.

Feel free to revise your strategy as you learn more about the issues. For instance, you may read a case with a related cause of action that you had not considered or you may encounter an article that highlights a relevant defense that you had not known of earlier. If so, you need to adjust your research accordingly.

When developing your research plan, the issue statement and research terms are the most crucial step toward conducting effective legal research. Brainstorm broadly to develop an expansive list of research terms. Refer to this list as you begin work in each new source. Note on the list which terms were helpful in which resource. Add new terms to the list as you discover them. This list is especially likely to grow during your initial efforts if you begin with a secondary source that provides context for the research project.

III. Conducting Your Research

A. Taking Notes and Keeping Organized

Take careful notes throughout the research process. Taking notes on your research can help you avoid duplicating steps, especially if you have to interrupt your research for a significant length of time. Research notes also provide a basis for organizing and writing your document. None of these notes have to be formal or typed, but they should at least be organized and readable.

The only "right" way to take notes and keep your research organized is the way that best helps you perform effective research, understand the legal issues, and analyze the problem. You may want to use index cards to note the authorities you consulted and what you found in them, and organize the cards chronologically or by type of authority. You could also write notes on a pad of paper or on your computer in a single document.

As you begin with each new resource, make notes that summarize your work in that resource. For print research, indicate the volumes you used, the indexes or tables you used, and the terms you searched for. For computer research, indicate the website or service, the specific database, and the searches you entered.[1] List both successful and unsuccessful index terms and searches so that you do not inadvertently repeat these same steps later, so that you can revisit a "dead end" that eventually becomes relevant, and so that you can return to a particularly successful search later and run it again to retrieve more current results.

Do not underestimate the learning process that occurs while taking notes. Deciding what is important enough to include in notes and expressing your reasoning in your own words will increase your understanding of the legal issues involved. Highlighting a printed document does not provide this analytical advantage.

However you choose to keep your notes, you will want one central place to organize copies or print outs of your most important authorities and documents. Although you may also want to keep electronic copies of these documents, you should be sure to have at least one copy in print as well.[2] Many people find that the most effective way to organize their research projects is to have a three-ring binder with tabs. Useful tabs can organize your research plan, research notes, citation list for all authorities, cases, statutes (and related authorities such as constitutional provisions or court rules), regulations, and secondary sources. Although this sort of research organization system may seem elaborate, keep in mind that you may be called off a project at any time. Someone else may need to take over for you if you

---

1. Taking notes on your computer will make recording your searches easier, as you can simply cut and paste the text of your searches from the search box and into your notes.

2. Having a copy in print will make it easier to provide copies to other people in your office who want to work with print, and will safeguard against computer and network crashes. Furthermore, having all of the authorities together in one place, where it is easy to see them together, may help your research and analytical process.

are directed to work on more urgent matters. That person will need to know exactly what you have done and what you found. Also, having all of your research steps and results in an organized and easily understandable notebook or other file system will not only impress your superiors and colleagues, it will make your research more efficient and streamlined, thus saving you time and frustration, and saving your client money.

B. Secondary Authorities

Write a brief summary for each secondary source you consult — even if it is just to record what search terms you used and the fact that you found nothing relevant. For the more fruitful sources, summarize in your own words the relevant analysis in the source. Always include references to specific pages or paragraphs. Try to include a few sentences about how this source relates to your research. Does it explain the background of a statute? Does it trace the development of a line of cases? Does it criticize the law in your jurisdiction? Does it suggest a novel approach to your problem? Additionally, note any references to primary authorities that may be on point. Remember that your goal is to leave an organized set of research notes that will enable someone new to the project to understand precisely what you have done and what you found without having to retrace your steps.

When working with secondary sources, resist the urge to press "print." The goals of reading secondary sources are usually to obtain an overview of an area of law and to locate citations to primary authority. These goals can be met by referring to secondary sources in the library or by skimming them online, without the waste of printing or copying numerous pages of text.

C. List of Authorities

Create a list of primary authorities that will contain the names and citations of all the authorities that you need to read. Devote one portion of the list to primary authorities and another portion to secondary authorities. Throughout your research, as you come across citations to potentially relevant authorities, include them in your list. This will allow you to maintain your train of thought with one resource while ensuring that you keep track of important cites to check later. If your list contains a number of entries, check for duplicates before reading the authorities.

D. Analytical Notes on Primary Authorities

At frequent points, stop and read the primary authority that you are finding. Legal analysis occurs throughout the process of researching a legal issue; reading as you research will ensure that you are finding relevant material.

Quickly read each authority first to decide whether it is relevant. Your goal here is not to understand every nuance of the document, but to make a decision as to whether it is definitely relevant, is definitely not relevant, or needs further consideration. Making this decision can be time consuming, especially for a novice legal researcher.

To determine the relevancy of statutes and rules, focus primarily on operative language that sets out duties or proscribes certain conduct. Move next to examine the parts of the statute that provide definitions. You should also browse through the statutory sections just before and after the most relevant parts to see if they have a bearing on your issue. Sections setting forth the purpose of the statute or that are plainly not applicable to your client's situation should just be briefly skimmed over.

To determine the relevancy of cases, begin by reading the synopsis at the beginning of the case. Then skim the headnotes or core concepts to find the portions of the case that appear to be most relevant, and read those parts of the case first. Finally, skim over the procedural history, the facts of the case, and analysis of possibly unrelated points of law.

If the source contains relevant material, make notes on your list of authorities. If it is not relevant, strike through it on your list. On your computer, you can use the "strike through" font mark-up tool to make this notation. Do not completely delete or erase irrelevant authorities; otherwise, you may later find yourself accidentally reading them again.

Once you have selected a number of relevant authorities, choose an organizational scheme for reading them carefully in groups. If there is a constitutional provision, statute, or rule on point, begin by reading it carefully, then move to reading cases that interpret the provision. One approach is to read cases in reverse chronological order, starting with the most recent. This approach lets you see the current state of the law first. You may find that the more recent cases summarize and explain the older cases, which will help you understand them and read them more efficiently. This approach also helps you avoid spending time learning old law that has been revised or superseded.

Reading cases chronologically may be time consuming for causes of action that have existed for many years. Except for historical research, you may want to impose an artificial cut-off of twenty or thirty years in the past so that you put your effort into recent law. Of course, you should always keep an open mind with respect to your cut-off: if you see hints that an older case may be particularly on point, you should read it carefully regardless of when it was decided.

After you have gone over all relevant authorities initially to assess their importance, you will want to read the more pertinent authorities slowly and carefully. Be sure you understand the procedural posture of each case, since this affects the standard of review applied. Also be sure that you understand the facts of cases. Drawing a timeline or chart of the relationships between the parties may be helpful. As you read through the opinions, cross out portions dealing with legal issues that are not confronting your client. If you decide that the case is not actually relevant or important, mark that on the first page so that you will not waste time reading it again.

When researching several issues or related claims, consider them one at a time. You may have several lists of authorities, one for each claim you are researching. In particularly complex matters, you may want to create a different binder for each claim.

1. Notes on Statutes

Because the exact words of statutes are so important, you should print,[3] photocopy, or electronically save the text of these provisions. If a statute is very short and clear, highlighting the pertinent portions may be sufficient for your purposes. If the statute is long, complex, or requires reference to several other statutory provisions, make a succinct outline of the statute. You should stress those parts of the statute that are most pertinent to your client's situation and note in your outline relationships with other code sections. Creating this outline will help you understand the statute and its application to the issue you are researching.

2 Notes on Cases

When you decide that a case is relevant, you should brief it. The brief does not have to follow any formal style. The brief for each case should highlight the key aspects of the case that are relevant for your research problem. Create a short summary of the pertinent facts, holding, and reasoning. You may choose to do this on your computer, creating a document or a page of a document for each case. You may prefer to write your summary in your legal pad or create an index card. Each case brief should include the following:

- *Citation.* Including the full citation will make writing the document easier because you will avoid referring back to the original. Include parallel cites in case the first reporter you check is not available in your library or within the online service that your firm subscribes to.
- *Facts.* Include only those facts that are relevant to your project.

---

3. Always be careful when printing statutes from an annotated code. Typically, the default mode of printing code provisions from either LexisNexis or Westlaw is to print not just the statute itself, but all associated annotations as well. For statutes that have been heavily litigated, printing without changing this default could result in a print job of several hundred pages. Depending on whether your subscription charges for printing by the page, line, or document, this could be a very costly mistake.

- *Procedural posture.* State the procedural posture of the case and note any information about the standard of review applied by the court.
- *Holding and reasoning.* Summarize the court's analysis. Again, address only those issues in the case that are relevant to your project. For example, if a case involves a tort claim and the issue of when expert testimony will be admitted in court, and you are researching only the tort issue, there is no need for you to study and summarize the court's reasoning on admission of expert witness testimony. Skim that section to be sure there is no relevant information lurking there, then ignore it.
- *Pinpoint pages.* For case information that you will cite in your written document, include the pinpoint cite. Be sure that the pinpoint is to the page in the reporter that you have been asked to cite in your document, not to a parallel reporter. Be very careful with this task when working with case opinions that you have printed from an online source, where pagination in different reporters is indicated solely by an asterisk or two.
- *Reflections.* Include your thoughts on the opinion: How do you anticipate using it in your analysis? Does it resolve certain issues for your problem? Does it raise new questions?
- *Updating information.* Each case brief should have a designated space for updating. Whether you use Shepard's or KeyCite, you must update each case that you use in your analysis.

E. Updating

You will likely find yourself updating at several points during the research process. Updating with Shepard's or KeyCite early in the process will lead you to other authorities on point. Updating before you begin to rely on an authority is critical: you must verify that each authority you include in your analysis is still "good law." Updating just before submitting a document ensures that nothing has changed while you were working on the project.

When updating, take your list of cited primary authorities to the citatory service that you plan to use. Update each authority, making notes on your case briefs and statute outlines as to when you updated authorities, whether the authorities are still respected, and what new sources you found. Recording the date of your updating search will be helpful for when you perform your final update just before submitting your document because you will only have to check citing sources that became available in the interim.

Printing lists of citations is an easy and efficient way to compare new citations with your list of primary authorities. Keep these lists in the updating section of your binder.

F. Outlining Your Analysis

Because the most effective research often occurs in conjunction with the analysis of your particular project, try to develop an outline that addresses your client's problem as soon as you can. If outlining feels too restrictive, you may benefit from a chart that organizes all the primary authority by issue or element, such as in Table 10-2, following the typical legal analysis format of Issue-Rule-Application-Conclusion (IRAC).

Your first analytical outline or chart may be based on information in a secondary source, the requirements of a statute, or the elements of a common law claim. It will become more sophisticated and detailed as you conduct your research. Recognize that you cannot reread every case or statute in its entirety each time you need to include it in your outline; instead, refer to your notes and briefs to find the key ideas supporting each step in your analysis.

The outline or chart should enable you to synthesize the law, apply the law to your client's facts, and reach a conclusion on the desired outcome. Applying the law to your client's facts may lead you to research issues that may not be apparent in your initial assessment of the situation.

G. Ending Your Research

One of the most difficult problems new researchers face is deciding when to stop researching. Often deadlines imposed by the court

Table 10-2. Sample Analysis Chart

Research Question: Is an employee entitled to unemployment compensation after being dismissed from employment because, due to problems with drug addiction, he twice was caught sleeping on the job and threatened the coworker who reported him to the supervisor on the second occasion?

Controlling Statute: Tenn. Code Ann. §50-7-303(b)

Issue	Case	Rule	Application	Conclusion
Is sleeping on the job "misconduct connected with ... work"?	Wallace	Excessive absenteeism may be the basis of a finding of misconduct, but that level of absenteeism is determined on a case-by-case basis.	Sleeping on the job may be analogous to absenteeism	Two instances of sleeping on the job probably will not amount to employee misconduct if the employee was tired due to illness or disability, unless the employee disregarded a warning concerning the conduct or additional circumstances contributed to the dismissal.
	Miotke	Repeated absences by an employee who ignored four warnings that absenteeism would result in termination constituted misconduct connected with employment, even though the absences were related to the employee's alcoholism.	Sleeping had occurred on only two occasions.	
	Trout	Absences due to illness do not constitute misconduct.	Sleeping on the job was related to drug addiction.	
Is threatening a coworker "misconduct connected with ... work?"	Armstrong	Misconduct must amount to a breach of duty owed to the employer. Threatening a co-worker did not amount to misconduct because the threat was not directed at a supervisor, the incident did not disrupt work, and the employee had not been warned that this type of conduct would result in his immediate discharge.	Employee threatened a co-worker, not a supervisor. Employee had not been warned that threatening co-worker would result in immediate discharge.	In these circumstances, a threat intended to prevent a co-worker from reporting the employee's sleeping on the job may amount to breach of a duty owed to the employer only if it materially interfered with the employer's business.

or a supervisor will limit the amount of time spent on a research project. The expense to the client will also be a consideration.

Apart from these practical constraints, most legal researchers want to believe that if they search long enough they will find a case or statute or article or *something* that answers the client's legal question clearly, succinctly, and definitively. Sometimes that happens, but usually it doesn't. So, if you do not experience that *Eureka!* moment of finding the exact answer summed up in one authority, how do you know when your research is over?

The strongest sign that you have come to at least an initial stopping point is that your research in various sources leads you back to the same authorities. For example, say you first find a good, explanatory secondary source. The secondary source cites to case opinions and statutes. You look up the statutes in an annotated code, and check the case annotations there. The cases summarized in the annotated code are the same cases that you found cited in the secondary source. Perhaps you find some cross-references to related statutes. You read those, and examine their case annotations. Again, the case summaries are of the same decisions to which you already have citations. You turn to reading the case opinions, and find that they all interpret and apply the statutes you have already read. You run the case citations through Shepard's or KeyCite, and find that the cases have been cited by some law review articles. You skim the law review articles, and find that they all cite to the case opinions and statutes you have already found. Eventually, your research seems to be leading you in a circle, back to where you have already been, rather than branching out to new authorities. This is a strong indication of the thoroughness of your research. As a final checklist, go through each step of the basic research process outlined in Chapter 1 to ensure you considered each one. Then review your research plan and notes on your research process to make sure that you have covered all of the issues presented to you.

When you are working online, knowing when to stop researching can be particularly difficult. Because you are jumping from link to link and database to database without moving from your computer, it is easier to lose track of where you have been online, and what you have seen, than if you are reading books in a library, and moving from one shelf to another, or one volume to another. This is where your careful note-taking will help you immensely. Also, be sure to make use of the "History" and "Research Trail" features on LexisNexis and Westlaw to review your past searches and viewed documents.

If you have worked through the research process and found nothing, it may be that nothing exists. Before reaching that conclusion, though, expand your research terms and look in a few more secondary sources. If you have not already done so, try looking at other jurisdictions to see if they have helpful persuasive authority. If they do, you could use it in your work directly, or you could see if it will help bring you closer to authority from your home jurisdiction that you did not find in your earlier research. For example, if you were originally researching Tennessee law, but could only find a relevant case opinion from Georgia, perhaps you would find better search terms within the Georgia case that you could use to refine your searching in a Tennessee case law database.

Remember that the goal of your research is to solve a client's problem. Sometimes the law will not seem to support the solution that your client had in mind. Think creatively to address the client's problem in a different way. While you must tell your supervisor or your client when a desired approach is not feasible, you will want to have prepared an alternate solution if possible.

Appendix A

Where to Find Tennessee Law

Tennessee Cases

Print sources:

West's South Western Reporter, Tennessee Decisions

- Summaries of some unpublished appellate cases are also available in *Tennessee Attorneys Memo*
- Very old Tennessee cases are available in miscellaneous reporters discussed in Chapter 2.

Free government website:

www.tsc.state.tn.us
- Opinions available going back to 1995/96
- Unofficial versions only

LexisNexis:

- To search: Select "States-Legal" menu, then "Tennessee," then from the "Cases" sub-menu, select "TN State Cases, Combined."
- Sample formats for retrieving a Tennessee case using Get a Document:
  136 S.W.2d 721
  2 Tenn. Ch. App. 132
  225 Tenn. 1.

Westlaw:

- To search: Enter TN in the "Search these databases" box to search combined Tennessee state court cases.
- Sample formats for retrieving a Tennessee case using Find:
  834 S.W.2d 915
  225 Tenn. 1.

Tennessee Constitution

Print source:

> *Tennessee Code Annotated* (Michie, official version), *West's Tennessee Code Annotated* (unofficial version)

Free websites:

- www.state.tn.us/sos/bluebook/online/section5/tnconst.pdf (.pdf version provided by the Tennessee Secretary of State)
- www.michie.com
  Scroll down and click on "Tennessee Code." From resulting page, select "Constitution" from left frame. Prior Tennessee Constitutions also available.

LexisNexis:

- To search: Select "States-Legal" menu, then "Tennessee," then from "Statutes & Regulations" sub-menu, click on "View More Sources," then "TN - Tennessee Constitution."
- Sample format to retrieve a constitutional provision using Get a Document:
  Tenn. Const. art. I @1

Westlaw:

- To search: Enter TN-STM-ANN (for the official Michie version) or TN-ST-ANN (for the unofficial West version) in the "Search these databases" box. Remove "-ANN" from the database identifier to search the unannotated version of the statutory code and constitution.
- Sample format to retrieve a Constitutional provision using Find:
  TN CONST Art. 1, s 1

Current Statutory Code

Print sources:

> *Tennessee Code Annotated* (Michie, official version), *West's Tennessee Code Annotated* (unofficial version)

Free website:

www.michie.com
- Scroll down and click on "Tennessee Code."
- Unannotated

LexisNexis:

- To search: Select "States-Legal" menu, then "Tennessee," then, from the "Statutes & Regulations" sub-menu, either select "Tennessee Code Annotated, Constitution, Court Rules & ALS Combined" or "Tennessee Code Annotated."
- Sample format to retrieve a current statute using Get a Document: tca 36-1-101

Westlaw:

- To search: Enter TN-STM-ANN (for the official Michie version) or TN-ST-ANN (for the unofficial West version) in the "Search these databases" box. Remove "-ANN" from the database identifier to search the unannotated version of the statutory code and constitution.
- Sample format to retrieve a current statute using Find:
  tn st 36-1-101
- (note that "Find" on Westlaw will always retrieve the unofficial version of the code. It is not possible to retrieve the official version of the code using "Find.").

Archival/Superseded Statutory Codes

Print sources:

- Check with your law library to see if it maintains archived versions in print or on microfiche.

Free website:

- None.

LexisNexis:

- To search: Select the "States-Legal" menu, then "Tennessee," then from "Statutes & Regulations" sub-menu, click on "View

More Sources," then "Legislative Archive," then select which year's code you want to search. Available back to 1991.
- It is not possible to use "Get a Document" to retrieve the archival version of a Tennessee statute.

Westlaw:

- To search: Enter TN-STMANNxx (where xx is the last two digits of the year's code you wish to search) in the "Search these databases" box. For example, TN-STMANN90 is the archived Tennessee Code Annotated for 1990. Available back to 1986.
- It is not possible to use "Find" to retrieve the archival version of a Tennessee statute.

Session Laws/Slip Laws

Print source:

Public and Private Acts of the State of Tennessee

Free government website:

http://tennessee.gov/sos/acts/
- Acts are arranged by law number and in searchable format back to 1997 (100th General Assembly).
- Indexes to most recent two legislative sessions are also usually available.

LexisNexis:

- To search: Select "States - Legal" menu, then "Tennessee," then from "Statutes & Regulations" sub-menu, click on "View More Sources," then "TN - Tennessee Advance Legislative Service." Use a date restrictor to search for session laws from a particular year. Available back to 1989.
- Sample format to retrieve a Tennessee session law using Get a Document:
1997 Tenn. Pub Acts 244

Westlaw:

- To search: Enter TN-LEGIS-OLD (for all session laws back to 1990) or TN-LEGIS (for slip laws from the current legislative session) in the "Search these databases" box. In TN-LEGIS-OLD, use a date restrictor in your search to retrieve only laws passed in a particular year.
- It is not possible to retrieve a Tennessee session law using "Find."

Administrative Regulations

Print source:

- Administrative regulations are not available in print.

Free government website:

www.tennessee.gov/sos/rules/
- This online version is the official version.
- The regulations are in .pdf format; they are not easily searchable.

LexisNexis:

- To search: Select "States - Legal" menu, then "Tennessee," then from "Agency & Administrative Materials" sub-menu, click on "View More Sources," then "TN - Rules & Regulations of the State of Tennessee"
- Sample format to retrieve a Tennessee regulation using Get a Document:
  Tenn. Comp. R. & Regs. R. 1720-4-6.01

Westlaw:

- To search: Enter TN-ADC in the "Search these databases" box to search the Tennessee administrative code.
- Sample format to retrieve a Tennessee regulation using Find:
  TN ADC 1720-4-6-.01

Administrative Register

Print source:

> Current *Tennessee Administrative Register* no longer available in print. Your law library may hold archival editions.

Free government website:

> www.tennessee.gov/sos/pub/tar
> - The online version is the official version.
> - The state version is typically more current than versions available elsewhere.

LexisNexis:

> - To search: Select "States-Legal" menu, then "Tennessee," then from "Agency & Administrative Materials" sub-menu, click on "View More Sources," then "TN - Tennessee Administrative Register."
> - Sample format to retrieve a page of the *Tennessee Administrative Register* using Get a Document:
> 27-7 Tenn. Admin. Reg. 132 (will retrieve page 132 of volume 27, issue no. 7).

Westlaw:

> The *Tennessee Administrative Register* is not available on Westlaw.

Tennessee Court Rules, Evidentiary Rules, Procedural Rules, and Professional Rules

Print sources:

> Tennessee court rules and professional rules are included in the "Rules" volumes of the *Tennessee Code Annotated* and *West's Tennessee Code Annotated*. The Rules of Professional Conduct for attorneys are found at Rule 8 in the Tennessee Supreme Court Rules. The Rules volumes also include selected Local Rules of Practice.

Free government website:

> www.tsc.state.tn.us/ and click on "Court Rules" link on left
> side of page.

- This site also includes links to proposed rules.
- Links to some local rules of practice are found here as well.

LexisNexis:

- To search: Select "States-Legal" menu, then "Tennessee," then, from the "Statutes & Regulations" sub-menu, select "TN - Tennessee Code Annotated, Court Rules, & ALS Combined" database. From the "Table of Contents" page displayed next, check the boxes for the sets of court rules you wish to search. Alternatively, choose "Tennessee," then under the "Statutes & Regulations" sub-menu, choose "View More Sources," then "Tennessee State & Federal Court Rules."
- It is not possible to retrieve individual court rules using "Get a Document."

Westlaw:

- To search: Enter TN-RULES in the "Search these databases" box for the database containing state and federal rules for Tennessee.
- To retrieve a Tennessee rule of court using "Find," type *tn rules* in the "Find by citation" box and click "Go." A page will be brought up with templates to use for retrieving rules from all of the different sets of Tennessee rules available on Westlaw.

Attorney General Opinions

Print source:

> *Opinions of the Attorney General of the State of Tennessee.* Ceased publication in 2000.

Free government website:

> www.attorneygeneral.state.tn.us/opyear.htm
- Searchable or browseable
- Available 1999 (partial) to present

LexisNexis:

- To search: Select "States-Legal" menu, then "Tennessee," then, from "Agency & Administrative Materials" sub-menu, select "TN Attorney General Opinions." Coverage starts in 1977.
- Sample format to retrieve a Tennessee Attorney General Opinion using Get a Document:
  10 Op. Atty Gen. Tenn. 1273
- This citation will retrieve the opinion found at page 1273 of volume 10 of the print series *Opinions of the Attorney General of the State of Tennessee.* "Get a Document" is available only for volumes 6–10 of the series.

Westlaw:

- To search: Enter TN-AG in the "Search these databases" box for the database that contains Tennessee Attorney General opinions. Coverage starts in 1977.
- Sample citation to retrieve a Tennessee Attorney General opinion using Find:
  Tenn. Op. Atty. Gen. No. 01-156
- Note that "01" in this sample citation refers to the year of publication (2001), noted as a two-digit number.

Appendix B

Selected Bibliography

General Research
(tending to focus on federal material)

Robert C. Berring, *Berring on Legal Research DVD* (Thomson/West 2006).

Robert C. Berring & Elizabeth A. Edinger, *Finding the Law* (12th ed. 2005).

Morris L. Cohen & Kent C. Olson, *Legal Research in a Nutshell* (8th ed. 2003).

Stephen Elias & Susan Levinkind, *Legal Research: How to Find and Understand the Law* (13th ed. 2005).

Christina L. Kunz et al., *The Process of Legal Research* (6th ed. 2004).

Roy M. Mersky & Donald J. Dunn, *Fundamentals of Legal Research* (8th ed. 2002).

Ruth Ann McKinney, *Legal Research: A Practical Guide and Self-Instructional Workbook* (4th ed. 2003).

Kent C. Olson, *Legal Information: How to Find It, How to Use It* (1999).

Amy E. Sloan, *Basic Legal Research: Tools and Strategies* (3d ed. 2006).

Tennessee Research

Simon C. Bieber et al., *Find it Free and Fast on the Net: Strategies for Legal Research on the Web* (2006).

Lewis L. Laska, *Tennessee Legal Research Handbook* (1977).

Steven R. Thorpe, "Uncovering Legislative History Resources in Tennessee," 31 Tenn. B.J. 18 (1995).

Specialized and Advanced Legal Research

J.D.S. Armstrong & Christopher A. Knott, *Where the Law Is: An Introduction to Advanced Legal Research* (2004).

Robert C. Berring, *Berring's Legal Research Podcasts,* http://www .berringlegalresearch.com/podcast.asp.

Prestatehood Legal Materials: A Fifty-State Research Guide, Including New York City and the District of Columbia (Michael Chiorazzi and Marguerite Most eds., 2005).

George Washington International Law Review, *Guide to International Legal Research* (2006).

Claire M. Germain, *Germain's Transnational Law Research: A Guide for Attorneys* (1991) (looseleaf).

Stacey L. Gordon, *Online Legal Research: A Guide to Legal Research Services and Other Internet Tools* (2003).

Specialized Legal Research (Penny A. Hazleton ed., 2003) (looseleaf).

William A. Raabe et al., *Federal Tax Research* (7th ed. 2006).

Texts on Legal Analysis

Charles R. Calleros, *Legal Method and Writing* (5th ed. 2006).

Linda H. Edwards, *Legal Writing: Process, Analysis and Organization* (4th ed. 2006).

Richard K. Neumann, Jr., *Legal Reasoning and Legal Writing: Structure, Strategy, and Style* (5th ed. 2005).

Laurel Currie Oates & Anne Enquist, *The Legal Writing Handbook: Analysis, Research, and Writing* (4th ed. 2006).

William H. Putman, *Legal Research, Analysis, and Writing* (2004).

David S. Romantz & Kathleen Elliott Vinson, *Legal Analysis: The Fundamental Skill* (1998).

Deborah S. Schmedemann & Christina L. Kunz, *Synthesis: Legal Reading, Reasoning, and Writing* (2d ed. 2003).

Helene S. Shapo et al., *Writing and Analysis in the Law* (rev. 4th ed. 2003).

About the Authors

Sibyl Marshall is the Head of Public Services at the University of Tennessee's Joel A. Katz Law Library.

Carol McCrehan Parker directs the Legal Writing Program at the University of Tennessee College of Law.

Index